T0195897

# One Step Back –
# Two Steps Forward

## The Dance of My Ultimate Plan

LeCount R. Davis, CFP®

**author**HOUSE®

AuthorHouse™
1663 Liberty Drive
Bloomington, IN 47403
www.authorhouse.com
Phone: 1 (800) 839-8640

Published by AuthorHouse  01/03/2020

ISBN: 978-1-7283-4108-8 (sc)
ISBN: 978-1-7283-4243-6 (hc)
ISBN: 978-1-7283-4107-1 (e)

Library of Congress Control Number: 2019921224

Print information available on the last page.

My parents, Henry and Daisy Davis, for loving, rearing, encouraging, and protecting me from hurt, harm, and danger.

My wife, Jewel W. Davis, for her love, companionship, and support.

My sister, Virginia Fletcher, for her love, protection, influence, and motivation.

My childhood community/village for their love, prayers, support, and motivation.

Mount Calvary Baptist Church, Rockville, Maryland, for spiritual nurturing and support.

Rev. Dr. Hiawatha B. Fountain for his unyielding spiritual support and counseling.

# Contents

# Foreword

This book is more than a record of the life and legacy of one black businessman in America. It chronicles the history, hopes, and struggles of the many whose voices and faces we will never know—and on whose shoulders we stand.

When I met LeCount R. Davis, he was already a highly successful man in the world of finance. He had power, prestige, and respect in his chosen profession. He was the go-to person in the African American community, domestically and internationally, including such places as the Bahamas, on matters of financial planning and building wealth.

A pioneer and trailblazer, LeCount was the first African American Certified Financial Planner in the United States. LeCount, one would think, had need of nothing. However, there was a searching in his spirit that caused me to ask, "What could be missing in a person's life who seemed to be at the top of his profession?" When we got to know each other better, it was evident to me what LeCount was searching for.

While attending a men's retreat about thirty years ago, I said, "LeCount, you are in church, but is church in you?"

He told me later that the interaction at the retreat was a turning point in his spiritual life. Great men are always better when they find and fill the God-shaped vacuum they are looking for.

Growing up in the shadow of the US Capitol in Washington, DC, at a time when many black men throughout the United States had their dreams deferred, LeCount kept his focus. He was destined for greatness at an early age.

As you read this book, you will discover that Mr. Davis epitomizes the definition of a Renaissance man, and his story can benefit all of us. I believe readers will find that the providential hand of a caring God is always at work with us.

I am honored to have been asked by my friend and spiritual brother, LeCount R. Davis, to write this foreword.

—Rev. Hiawatha B. Fountain, PhD, retired associate superintendent, Montgomery County Public Schools, Maryland, and spiritual advisor for men's fellowship, Mt. Calvary Baptist Church, Rockville, Maryland

# Acknowledgments

Special acknowledgement is given to Robert Louis Shepard, PhD, author of the highly acclaimed *Fulfilling My Destiny, Step by Step (AuthorHouse, 2013; The Shepard Institute (TSI), LLC, 2016)* and an accompanying self-help guide *(TSI, LLC, 2017)* for the consultancy service he provided on the production of this book. His detailed review of the draft manuscript to ready it for publication in book form and his interaction with the publishing company on my behalf was invaluable.

Special thanks also go out to Rev. Dr. Hiawatha B. Fountain, spiritual advisor, Herbert J. Miller (deceased), Mr. Payne (deceased), Judge Lucy B. Warr, attorney Arthur M. Reynolds Sr., Benjamin L. King Sr. CPA (deceased), Alexandra Armstrong, CFP®, and Major General Robert N. Ginsburgh, PhD, CFP® (deceased).

# Introduction

I was born in Washington, DC, and graduated from Armstrong High School in 1954—the year the US Supreme Court declared that segregated schools were unconstitutional. I grew up in a ghetto that was spiritually rich but financially and economically poor. My dad was a day laborer and poured concrete for a living. He had to pursue odd jobs to make enough money to take care of his family. When the weather was too cold, rainy, or snowy, his earning decreased drastically. My mother stayed home to care for the children most of the time, and she worked as a domestic when called upon. Even when times were tough and money was short, we took advantage of the opportunities to help our neighbors.

My mother often cooked meals for the sick and shut-in, and my father did minor repairs to neighborhood houses and furniture, requesting no compensation. The children shoveled snow and took out the trash when a neighbor could not do those chores. Many of our neighbors also did good deeds on a daily basis. That's how our village made it in those days.

The more things change, the more they stay the same. I believe God's blessings, His love, and caring for and helping others are our hope for survival and prosperity. I chose my financial planning and advisory career based on that belief. Without God's grace and blessings, I could do nothing but fail. I wanted to help others achieve and meet their goals by passing on His blessings to others according to His Works, Will, and Word. I walked by faith and the belief that He would take care of my family and me. Many black people who did not know or believe in God had little hope that things would ever change. This mind-set often resulted in a circle of poverty, disappointment, frustration, and despair.

We had a saying in the village that when you "kill the head, the body dies." This meant that a lack of hope eliminates aspiration and motivation. My parents and my village did not want me to be influenced by what others decided I would be. I was taught many years ago that a lack of money should not determine my class category.

Class should not depend on money or wealth; it should depend on how you live your life according to God's Works, Will, and Word. If my economic status is classified as middle class, would you classify most of my people as low class? That is how many people view us. I was taught that I might have been "low income" but "high class" since we are all in God's sight.

With my hands in God's hand, I believe nothing is impossible. I want others to see that what He has done for me, He will do for anyone who opens the doors of their heart and lets him in.

After some prodding from my spiritual advisor Rev. Dr. Hiawatha Fountain, Deacon Dr. Robert Shepard, other church members, and financial planning peers and associates,

I decided to write this book. Every year, I made a financial planning presentation at my church's men retreat.

At one of the retreats, after hearing my presentation, which included my past and my spiritual motivation, Deacon Kohn said that my story deserved to be put out in book form. That was when I started thinking seriously about writing this book.

I was led by the Holy Spirit to pursue my life's vision and mission, and this book is a way to pass on my beliefs, experiences, and ideas for success. I pray that I can be a beacon of light for aspiring financial planners and advisors in helping our communities become better stewards in handling money.

Mr. Payne, the community financial and tax guru, gave me my initial inspiration and motivation to pursue a career in accounting and finance. I will elaborate more on this in chapter 2.

If this book can help just one person, my purpose and efforts will not be in vain. Everyone has a story, and this is mine. It is the dance of God's ultimate plan for me.

Rev. Dr. Hiawatha B. Fountain and I discussing
the relationship of money and the Bible

# Chapter 1

# The Power of Faith and Belief

God knew me before I knew Him. I know now that He had plans for me, and I believe He never will leave or forsake me. In my youth, I spent so much time in church that some people believed I would become a minister.

My spiritual advisor, Rev. Dr. Hiawatha Fountain, said, "You were in the church, but the church was not in you."

When I took a step back and reflected on God's blessings, Rev. Fountain was right. I could not ignore God's Love, Power, Works, Will, and Word after reflecting on how His blessings manifested to me in the saving of my life three times. God was, is, and always will be my GPS. When I'm going in the wrong direction, He redirects me so I can reach my intended destination. He is a light unto my feet and a lamp unto my pathway. God is the choreographer of the dance of my ultimate plan.

When I was in the third grade, I was hit in the head with a wayward stone from a schoolmate on the playground. I was stretched out on the ground and bleeding profusely with the rock embedded in my skull.

My teacher was summoned and took me to the nearest hospital, which was three or four blocks from the playground. The hospital did not accept blacks and would not admit me for treatment. My teacher told the hospital attendant that if I was denied hospital services and died, she would launch a public relations campaign to expose their refusal to admit me.

The hospital still did not admit me, but they patched me up and sent me to Freedmen's Hospital (now Howard University Hospital) for admission. I was told I was twenty to thirty minutes from death when I arrived at Freedman, the hospital designated for blacks at that time. "He promised He would never leave me nor forsake me," and God is a promise keeper.

The second time I took a step back and reflected on His blessings was when I was sent home from Wilberforce University because of a "suspected" medical condition that the university could not handle. My Wilberforce experience is elaborated on in a later chapter. I believe I had a medical problem, and on the bus ride back to Washington, God removed it. After numerous x-rays, procedures, and examinations, no medical problem was ever found.

The third time I took a step back and recognized His blessing of saving me from death was when I was late for a business meeting in South America. When we arrived for the meeting, I was told that guerillas had shot up the boardroom where the meeting was to be held. I was told that if I had been on time, it is a possibility that I would not have written this book. "He said He would never leave me nor forsake me."

Others may have different interpretations of these three incidents, but I walk by faith and belief in God and know He saved me three times because He had an ultimate plan for me.

Life's journey is never a straight line. There have been times of joy and jubilation and times of adversities, heartaches, and disappointments. One's life journey is like a dance; you take steps back to reflect on your blessings, learn from the past, and take steps forward to reap the benefits of God's ultimate plan for you. So, let the dance begin.

My sister Virginia Fletcher and my mother Daisy Davis

# Chapter 2

# The Early Years

Taking a step back, I can only imagine what my father had to go through to provide for his family. I was the fifth of eight children in a blended family and the middle child of the three children birthed by Henry and Daisy Davis. My father was born in Spartanburg, South Carolina. I was thirty years old when he died, and he never complained about his trials, struggles, or tribulations. He just worked hard and did what he had to do.

Sometimes he worked on multiple jobs that prevented him from spending family time with us to pass on his wisdom, inspiration, and guidance. He often left home before we woke and returned home after we were asleep. He was so tired that he went to bed after gulping down some food. He never attended the many activities of my sister and me: boxing matches, table tennis tournaments, and dance contests. He was just too tired from working multiple jobs to support the family to enjoy the success and participation of his children.

But in the times he found to talk to us, he never failed to inquire about the outcomes of our activities. He stayed on top of who our friends were and cautioned us to stay out of trouble. My younger sister and I never got in trouble and did not cause our parents any grief or pain. We were always studying, working, and doing positive things in the neighborhood in any ways we could.

When we needed food, we depended on the grocery store next door. The proprietor kept an accounts payable book to record when we purchased food when my father was unemployed or weather conditions prevented him from working. He gave us credit until my father was able to pay his debt. Quite naturally, the debt was always higher than the cost of the food we purchased. We now call that interest.

My father did what he had to do to keep food on the table, but the food tab was for food for his family and neighbors who needed it. We did not have the best of clothing, but we were always warm, clean, and presentable. My mother saw to that. The rent was always paid, and we were never evicted or homeless. With God's blessings, my father always provided for all our needs. He died on April 16, 1968, at 4:30 p.m. in Freedmen's Hospital.

Through it all, my mother was a pillar of strength and carried on as best she could. With God's blessings, my sister and I provided for her needs. My mother was born in Fayetteville, North Carolina, on January 1, 1899, went on to glory on July 6, 1983, at the age of eighty-four. She moved in with my sister, Virginia, and lived with her until her passing.

Mom was a quiet and unassuming woman who loved my father and their children with compassion and strength.

She was always there for us—even when my father could not make it because of his heavy work commitments.

For some reason, she never suggested that her children even visit Fayetteville probably because she had too many horrible memories. She told us stories about our grandmother Della who also must have had a terrible time living and raising a family in Fayetteville. Grandmother Della use to kid her about naming me LeCount, and when visiting us, she would never call me by that name. When asked how she came up with the name, Mom explained that I was named after the doctor who delivered me (Dr. LeCount Matthew). To Grandma, my name was "Hezekiah of the Bible." Families from that era and location were very religious and worshiped God without limitation. Later in life, I was reading the Bible and found out Hezekiah was a king. Maybe Grandma felt that God had his hands on me and thought I would be something special in His sight—maybe even a king.

My sister always complained to my parents that they were spoiling me. Because I was a picky eater, my mother would cook two meals: one for me and another for the other members of the family. My sister would always say, "Why don't you make him eat the same meal everyone else is eating?"

I was given additional time to study, play sports, and participate in outside activities.

The household chores and duties fell on my sister because Henry Jr. was never around. Whatever happened around the house seemed to unconsciously revolve around me. Despite what they had to go through, I never saw my parents fussing or fighting. I'm sure they did, but they didn't do it in front of the children. My father always treated mom with utmost respect and realized her contribution in raising us and stabilizing our family.

When I was in high school, in a motherly way, she said, "Son, you have plenty of book sense, but in order to make it in this world, you need some common sense."

My life and future were based on that advice. My financial television show, mentioned later in this book, was entitled *Common Cents,* which was taken from her advice.

My younger sister, Virginia, and I were very close in my youth. Although, one year younger, she became a surrogate mother who protected me from the negative influences in DC. We attended church and parties together. I often tagged along with her and her boyfriend—an excellent dancer—to parties and dance contests.

She did not actively participate in sports, but she came to see me play. She did, however, beat me several times at table tennis at the neighborhood settlement house.

She taught me how to type and led me to a clerk-typist position at the US Patent Office. While she worked there, she met her husband, Edward Fletcher. She was disappointed when I married too early, but she continued to support me in any way she could. Even after my marriage to Jewel, we stayed in contact to see how we were coping with and enjoying life.

Virginia was a saver who kept her expenses in check and did not believe in credit card debt. After I received a large sum of money from a business deal, I often called to see if she needed anything. She looked at me in astonishment and said, "Do *you* need anything?" She told me that she had saved quite a bit of money and had more than she needed. She predeceased me and went home to glory on March 7, 2016. I will always miss her and her motherly and guiding hand. My parents and sister were like angels who God sent to build a fence around me and protect me.

I was a good, not outstanding, student in elementary, junior high, and high school. All of my teachers were very attentive to their students and took exceptional amounts of time to tell us about the history and legacy of black people and motivate us in our pursuit of an education and a prosperous life—regardless of our economic situations. Their counseling was invaluable and taught us how important it was to love God, ourselves, and our families and to do unto others as we would have them do unto us. When I entered Armstrong High, I was more focused on sports than academics, but I later realized that a good education was the best path for me to follow.

Attending Armstrong High was a major step forward in my ultimate plan. It operated as an important institution and a symbol for the African American community in Washington, and it helped improve the quality of life for its students.

In the mid-nineteenth century, the District of Columbia emerged as a national model for educating African Americans. At the end of the nineteenth century, college preparatory institutions for African Americans came under attack.

Booker T. Washington led a campaign for vocational training of African Americans. He argued that training in agricultural, technical, and business instruction—as opposed to the arts and humanities—would ensure racial progress. Armstrong High School, formerly known as M Street High School, successfully resisted the pressure to turn the school into a trade school. In 1925, the school was renamed

Armstrong Technical High School. (DC designation May 23, 1996; National Register listing August 16, 1996 ;DC Ownership)

From the beginning, the expressed purpose of the school was to offer a combined course in academics and technical training. There was a double objective of preparing students to enter scientific and technical schools of college-grade and normal schools and to prepare students to immediately begin scientific and industrial pursuits.

Tech's memorable legacy involved scholars, artists, architects, doctors, dentists, engineers, military personnel, and athletes who became known locally, nationally, and internationally.

Elizabeth Chandler Yancey, Class of 1941, Vice Superintendent, DC Public Schools (Retired)

The class of 1954 conformed to Armstrong's original purpose. The school established an architect and engineering college preparatory program for college-bound students in our class of 1954. Many students in our class were outstanding scholars and high achievers in many academic and technical pursuits. Examples of the class's success include:

John Malachi

After graduation from Armstrong, John Malachi attended Purdue University and obtained a BS degree in electrical engineering. After a four-year tour in the air force as a ground electronics officer, he had a thirty-year career as an engineer and manager with the federal government, including twenty years at NASA as a spacecraft engineer. At NASA, he worked on the *Apollo* and communication satellite programs. After retiring from NASA, he worked for twenty years as a professor at Montgomery College.

## Dr. Omega C. Logan Silva, MD, MACP

Dr. Silva graduated cum laude from Howard University in 1956 with honors in chemistry and earned an MD in 1967. She is professor emeritus of medicine at George Washington University in Washington, DC. Dr. Silva is a long-standard advocate for universal health care and a committed supporter of the advancement of women in medicine. She was given a letter of commendation from President Reagan in 1984 and a letter of thanks from President Clinton in 1995 for her participation in health care reform. Dr. Silva has made numerous media appearances to raise awareness of women's health issues, including smoking, cervical cancer, and thyroid disease. In 1983, she was elected president of the Howard University Medical Alumni Association, making her the first woman to hold that post.

## Dr. Charles C. Kidd Sr.

Dr. Kidd excelled in technical sciences, earning a scholarship to Case Institute of Technology in Cleveland, Ohio, where he received an undergraduate degree in civil engineering. After completing his military service as an officer in the US Air Force, he entered the University of Michigan's College of Engineering and School of Public Health, where he received an MS in radiological health sciences, an MSE in civil engineering, and a PhD in environmental health sciences.

He served as a member of the faculty at University of Michigan as an assistant professor of radiological health. He served as the president of Olive Harvey College and vice president at Chicago State University. In order to pursue his passion of fostering the education of black youth, Dr. Kidd accepted a position as dean of the College of Engineering, Sciences, Technology, and Agriculture at Florida A&M University in Tallahassee. He subsequently became dean of graduate studies at Bethune Cookman University, and he helped develop the curriculum and programming for the School of Graduate and Professional Studies. (The Chaka Chinyelu Foundation, Inc. December 14, 2012.)

The Honorable John A. Burroughs Jr.

Ambassador John A. Burroughs Jr. earned his BA degree in political science from the University of Iowa in 1959 where he was an honorable mention All-American tackle. Upon graduation, the Philadelphia Eagles drafted him. After his brief stint with the Eagles, Mr. Burroughs was employed by the US Department of State and rose to become special assistant to the assistant secretary of the navy for manpower and reserve affair. Mr. Burroughs was awarded a Merrill Trust Fellowship to attend the Stanford Executive Program at Stanford University in Palo Alto, California. He also was awarded the Department of State's Superior Service Award by the undersecretary of management for his efforts in bringing about an increase in the number of minorities and women in the Foreign Service Officer Corps.

Mr. Burroughs was selected US ambassador to the Republic of Malawi and later was assigned as consul general in Cape Town, South Africa. He was appointed US ambassador to Uganda. Mr. Burroughs was a diplomat-in-residence at Lincoln University in Oxford, Pennsylvania. He was appointed as special coordinator for Sudan, primarily responsible for coordinating humanitarian assistance to that country.

On June 1, 1996, he was awarded the distinguished alumni achievement award by the University of Iowa Alumni Association.

Armstrong was well known for its athletics, and we were arguably the best in all the sports popular with blacks, including basketball, football, baseball, and track. I had the pleasure of playing baseball and basketball with one of the most remarkable athletes I ever knew. Gary Mays Sr. played both sports spectacularly—even though he had only one arm. Spingarn High had the best basketball player to come out of Washington: NBA Hall of Fame inductee Elgin Baylor. The only way we could compete with Spingarn was to stop Elgin, and guess who our coach assigned to slow him down? Gary Mays, the "One Arm Bandit."

Gary was a participant in a professional baseball tryout at Griffith Stadium. He was the most valuable player at that tryout and the most outstanding player of the tryouts. He did not play professional baseball because scouts thought his ability to throw out professional players would be limited, if not impossible, when they attempted to steal bases. They wanted him to change his position to the outfield, which he refused to do.

In high school, I drew the interest of some Major League scouts. Every kid in my village wanted to be Jackie Robinson, and I was no exception. I played second base for my high school team and thought I was pretty good. I was also invited to the tryout at Griffith Stadium where the "Black Babe Ruth," Josh Gibson, played for the Homestead Grays. I remember the remarks (and criticism) that one of the scouts made after seeing me fielding ground balls. He said I could make all the fancy backhand stops and throws, but I could not make the routine and fundamental plays. Since I was just an average batter, I could not compensate for that deficiency. I tried to make the necessary adjustments, but I didn't and was unsuccessful in my only Major League sport trials.

# Chapter 3

# It Takes a Village

In my close-knit community, we looked after each other. I remember a neighbor sitting at her front window and making sure we behaved and were safe as we went to and from school. My father gave a standing invitation to the neighbors to reprimand any of his children if they saw us misbehaving and then to tell him when he got home from work. He would then discipline us again.

Virginia and I were never disciplined, but my brother was. We were taught to always listen to, obey, and respect our elders, especially the preachers and teachers. Why is all this important? Because it was necessary to provide a proper foundation for children when we were young, and when we grew old, we would not stray from it. We are products of our rearing, teaching, exposure, and the care we received when we were very young.

My neighborhood played a vital role in raising me. The children took odd jobs to increase the household income when needed. My youth, through high school, was confined to a five-to-eight-block radius in the inner city of Washington.

Practically every family need, except for jobs, was attainable within my village. The grocery store was next door to my house. The church was within three blocks. Elementary through high school was within three blocks, and the neighborhood settlement house was only a block away. The settlement houses were equivalent to today's community centers, and kids went there to play games, go to sponsored summer camps, receive necessary counseling, and find a place to study.

I frequented the local boys club and YMCA, which were five and eight blocks from home, respectively. I often studied and did homework at the church. At the boys club and YMCA, I participated in several sporting events and received valuable counseling. I played basketball and baseball, and I was a featherweight boxer.

At the boys club, I developed many of my athletic skills that led to my basketball scholarship to Wilberforce. I boxed because my brother thought it was necessary to protect my sister and myself. My sister didn't need my protection. I was not that good at boxing, but the advice worked because no one bothered us. My brother fought enough to scare away any troubling youths. Television and mass media were not problems in our household because we only had a radio. Since we had no automobiles, we had to walk to our various destinations.

Several elders counseled and provided me with guidance that I will never forget. My parents practically turned me over to my village's counselors and sports coaches for protection and guidance. They always felt we were safe in their care and with their guidance.

My counselors included Mr. Jabbo Kenner, the Police Boys Club counselor and former heavyweight boxer, and Mr. Reginald Ballard Sr., an outstanding athlete and a Morgan State graduate. They treated every child in their care as their own. They saw that I did not get involved with the wrong crowd and stayed out of trouble, which was prevalent in my neighborhood. They emphasized the importance of education and kept me busy after school in many activities.

Their strategy worked. Mr. Ballard taught me that you play basketball defense with your feet—and that dancing would help my athletic movements. I took his advice, and as a side benefit, with the help of my sister, I became an excellent dancer. My sister and I won dancing contests all over the DC area. I even became proficient in ballroom dancing.

Our community settlement house counselor, Mr. Robinson, required us to do our homework before we were allowed to play any games. He took extreme time to talk to us, giving us the benefits of his life's experience, and he was always concerned about the welfare of our families. He taught me the importance of education and how it could be the doorway to being able to get employment and take care of my family. In every case, my village and counselors believed that if I stayed busy doing positive things, I would not have time to do negative things. At the Northwest Settlement House, I became a ping-pong champion in my age bracket, and I was a pretty good pool player.

As I grew older, other neighbors showed compassion and willingness to guide and counsel my sister and me. Mr.

Payne hired Virginia to provide typing and administrative help for his bookkeeping and tax preparation small business accounting practice. She convinced him to hire me also for minor clerical duties.

That was my introduction to income taxes and accounting services, which started me on my career path. Mr. Payne was the financial and tax guru for the entire neighborhood. When we had financial and income tax problems, we could always call on him for advice and guidance, and his influence led me to pursue an accounting education, which became an integral part of my ultimate plan. His dedication and willingness to help the community and those in need left a lasting impression on me. He told me that we had to always face the tax man—the IRS—and assistance in the preparation of income tax returns would always be needed.

Seeing the anguish on the faces of my neighbors when they came for their income tax preparation seem to confirm his belief that people would always need tax advice and assistance. I also saw the joy and gratitude on their faces when he listened and provided fundamental advice to deal with their financial concerns and problems. Years later, I decided to take his advice and pursue an accounting education.

Although I lived within walking distance of Howard, I had my sights fixed on the University of Maryland and sought an athletic scholarship there. That didn't work out too well, and my parents could not pay for my education. I had to stay local and work to help with the household expenses. I wanted to go to the University of Maryland, stay close to home, and ultimately make it in the pros, but that was not God's plan.

I graduated in 1954, which was when the US Supreme Court decided on *Brown v. the Board of Education*. Maryland was not ready to accept black athletes, which caused me much distress. I was so disappointed that I did not pursue any other colleges. While I was pouting and feeling sorry for myself, I began hanging out with the boys and working meaningless jobs to help out at home. In stepped my choreographer, God, and He sent one of his angels to rescue me.

A young recruiter, Mr. Brooks, from Wilberforce University in Ohio was looking for good basketball players and Washington was known for its athletes. I remember him driving up to the neighborhood hangout corner and seeing who my "friends" were. Having talked to my coach and several players, he told me I was not hangout material and that I better leave the corner alone and get an education if I wanted to survive. He cautioned me that an idle mind is the devil's workshop. After several informal workouts, he proceeded to get me a basketball scholarship to Wilberforce.

# Chapter 4

# Wilberforce, Here I Come

Wilberforce is located in Wilberforce, Ohio, and is affiliated with the African Methodist Episcopal (AME) Church. It is one of the nation's oldest Historically Black Universities and Colleges (HBCU). It was the first college to be owned and operated by African Americans. Wilberforce was established 1856 as a joint venture with the Methodist Episcopal Church.

A large crowd came to the bus station to see me off the day I left for Wilberforce. I was the first in my family to graduate from high school. I was also the first child I knew in my neighborhood to go to college; to them, it was a big deal. I was so motivated. I felt like I was carrying the hopes and aspirations of my village to school with me, and I was determined not to let them down.

I was apprehensive and hesitant as to how I would adjust to being away from home and my village. Other than visiting a relative in Brooklyn, New York, I had never left my village except to go to summer camp and other neighborhoods to play sports. *How should I act? What should I expect from my fellow students?* In stepped my choreographer, God, to show me the way again.

Entering the doors of Wilberforce University, I felt like I was returning to my roots and that God was telling me something—and that I had better listen. In the dormitory hall, I constantly heard students preparing for their Bible lessons and practicing delivery of their mock sermons. I did not know that a great number of the students who came to Wilberforce aspired to be ministers.

My first task was to make the basketball team. I thought I could handle the academics because I was a good student in high school. I quickly found out that Washington was not the only place where athletes knew how to play basketball. The Midwest produced some very good players too. I was good, but a guard from Chicago was better and won the starting guard position on our team. After an ego check, I settled in as his backup. That was the bad news. The good news was I had to realize not to depend on playing pro ball and concentrate more on my studies, which I did.

When I decided to concentrate on academics instead of sports, I also decided to join a Greek letter fraternity. After some discussions with other boys, I chose the Alpha Phi Alpha fraternity, which had the reputation of being the smartest fraternity on campus. After completing my probationary period as a Sphinx, I had to go through the customary hazing to become an Alpha man. I did not do well during the hazing process. My actions caused others to think that being from Washington meant I thought I was too good to go through the hazing process. I was immediately determined unfit to be an Alpha and never joined a fraternity.

I got hurt my first year and saw even less action than I anticipated. While making a spin move to the basket, I tried to hook my defender, but he had moved out of the way. I separated my left shoulder and was sent to the school nurse. Upon examination for the injury, it was determined that I had a serious unrelated medical problem and was told I had to return home to deal with it.

Being completely crushed, I returned home to get a second medical opinion. How could I face my family, my village, and my friends? After numerous examinations, including multiple x-rays, the doctors in Washington told me that I had no medical problems. They warned me about taking any further radiation exams and explained that too much exposure to radiation was dangerous. I followed the doctors' advice. As I mentioned in the first chapter, I believe I had a medical problem while at Wilberforce, but on the journey home, God, my choreographer, eliminated it because it was not part of His ultimate plan for my life.

After discovering that good news, I was faced with the decision of whether to return to Wilberforce or not. Since I would no longer have a basketball scholarship, my family could not afford my education costs. Further, they needed help in meeting the household expenses. I decided to get a job to help out.

The more things change, the more they stay the same. Many young men had to make the same decision before and never returned to school to finish their education. God saw that abandoning my education was not in His plan, and I got a federal government job and continued my education in Washington, but trouble was lurking.

# Chapter 5

# A Major Misstep

My ultimate plan was immediately in jeopardy when I made a major misstep in my life. I got married at the early age of nineteen, had four children before finishing my education, and faced an uncertain future. This situation started, as many others did, in my village. My first wife was attractive, and practically everybody in the village liked her.

I was the one in the village who had the most potential and best capability for getting a good job and raising a family my neighbors could only hope for. So, it was decided that we were a perfect match. It may sound stupid now, but in my village, boys became men and breadwinners as early as eighteen—and sometimes earlier.

Getting married too young usually begins the cycle of poverty and despair that leads to the social and financial problems my people face today. Recognizing our mistake of getting married too young led us to a divorce.

Insufficient income to support a family and the inability to pursue a meaningful education to improve one's economic conditions cause many to take drastic actions. I took a step back and recalled the fact that my father was a good family provider, worked hard, and lived a righteous life without a formal education, and I was determined that I would not fall prey to the negatives that could result from my missteps. God had already decided that to do so was not in His ultimate plan for my life.

Like my dad, I was always a good provider. So, I went back to school because my best chance of solving this problem was by acquiring an education. My busy work and travel schedule took away valuable family time. We decided that it would be best for the children to remain with their mother who was to provide full-time care and the necessary guidance for our young children.

I supplied all financial support, spent time with the children, and stayed a part of their daily lives. I tried to be the best absentee father I could, but I have to admit my efforts seemed like too little, too late. After several years, my wife became ill and felt unprepared to continue caring for our children. Their care now was totally on me. I had to integrate full-time fatherhood with work and educational goals. Better-paying employment was of utmost importance, and I needed more education to increase my income.

I enrolled in Southeastern University, which had a reputation for preparing students for employment in the federal government. I excelled in my studies and received both a bachelor's degree and a master's degree in accounting while supporting my family and being the best father I could be under the circumstances. While attending Southeastern, I worked as a clerk-typist and file clerk at the US Patent Office.

With the support and encouragement of my "little" sister, I continued to study and move forward. And with God's blessings and guidance, I made it. I had many sleepless nights. I again stepped back and remembered and believed the lyrics of a gospel song: "I lay awake at night, but that's all right. My God is going to fix it after a while." And He did.

Accounting jobs, even in the federal government, were few for blacks, so I started as an accounting clerk at the Federal Housing Administration (FHA) after graduation from Southeastern. I worked my way up to the supervisory position of that division and later was promoted to the position of internal auditor. Internal auditing is basically management accounting, which became very important to me as I climbed the ladder in the financial advisory industry.

While I was at FHA, I met and married Jewel Waller. I consider her my dance partner, and we began to take two steps forward together. Because she has meant so much to me in my life's journey and my career, I have devoted a chapter in this book to show how monumental those two steps forward were.

Author and wife at home

# Chapter 6

# I Found Me an Angel

After several successful years working in the federal government and moving up the career ladder, I decided to enter the private sector and use my experience and training to help people and small businesses improve their economic conditions. To accomplish this goal, I had to "find me an angel."

I was progressing well in my jobs and taking advantage of the opportunities I was blessed with, but I was wandering through life like a robotic nomad in the desert. I had no specific long-term goals or guidance on how I might achieve those goals. Well, that changed at the FHA when I ascended to the rank of supervisor of a team in the Multifamily Mortgage Section.

When managers decided on new hires, a young lady by the name of Jewel Elizabeth Waller applied and was hired in my section. She was beautiful inside and outside, very smart, and a very hard worker with a pleasant personality. She was the smartest employee on the team, and she was full of ambition and aspirations. We dated and found that we had many things in common.

Jewel was a native of Richmond, Virginia, and came from a loving and Christian family. She had an older brother and was the oldest of five girls. Jewel cared for other people and enjoyed facing challenges head-on. While growing up, she worked in her family-owned jewelry store. The family business, now under the leadership of her brother Richard, exists today after more than 118 years. Jewel credits her grandfather for her entrepreneurial spirit.

Jewel attended Virginia Union University in Richmond and was a popular student. She was selected for the Alpha Kappa Mu Honor Society, joined the Alpha Kappa Alpha sorority, and was voted "Miss Virginia Union University 1960." She received a Bachelor of Science degree (with honors) in business education in 1961. A year later, she relocated to Washington to accept the position with the FHA.

After a couple of years on my accounting team, Jewel accepted a promotion to the Internal Revenue Service as a personnel management specialist. She was then selected for the IRS's prestigious Management Intern Program, becoming the first African American female in the program.

During this time, I thought of the lyrics to Aretha Franklin's "Angel": "Got to find me an angel to fly away with." My first marriage was not so great. Had I learned enough to get it right the second time? Considering the "package" I would be bringing to the table, I was unsure that Jewel would accept my proposal. After all, she had to interrupt her career path, which was very promising, and defer some of the enjoyment life offered. God knew I needed a helpmate to fulfill my ultimate plan and sent me a "Jewel." So, we decided to take those infamous two steps forward together. Our coworkers called our marriage a merger because of the blending of our life's goals, aspirations, and approach to achieving success in whatever we desired.

In 1965, we were married in a beautiful wedding in Richmond. Her uncle, Rev. John B. Henderson, performed the ceremony. Jewel seamlessly moved into the role of the caring mother of my four children. In 1970, we moved into our beautiful spacious new contemporary home in Potomac, Maryland. At the time, moving into such a home was quite an accomplishment for two young people, and it was a testament to our faith and willingness to pursue our dreams.

For years, Jewel was very involved in the children's growth and development, nurturing, supporting, and guiding them from their preteen years through their college years. The entire family was socially active. They enjoyed traveling, attending concerts, sporting events, and other cultural and fun activities.

With our emphasis on education, we were able to provide three of our children a good college education. LeCount Jr. studied at the University of California Berkley and in Paris, France. He graduated from Middlebury College in Vermont, with a bachelor's and a master's degree in French civilization. Garland graduated from West Texas State University in Canyon, Texas, with a bachelor's degree in accounting. He received a football scholarship, was a student-athlete, and graduated in four years. He was later employed by the Dallas school system as an internal auditor. Garland passed away in Tucson, Arizona, due to a train accident at the age of thirty-two. Garland had been following in my footsteps as a student-athlete, receiving degrees in accounting, and working as an internal auditor.

Our oldest daughter, Felandria, attended Morgan State University in Baltimore, Maryland, and had a medical problem that interrupted her college education. Our youngest daughter, Michelle, graduated from the College of William & Mary in Williamsburg, Virginia. She met and married a young man who also graduated from William & Mary, and they have three children and one grandchild.

While working in the federal government and for an international labor organization and a certified public accounting firm, I still retained the vision of helping people thrive in an ever-growing and complex financial world. After much discussion with Jewel, she encouraged me to do what I believed in and to pursue my goal of self-employment and becoming a Certified Financial Planner. She supported me all the way and continues to provide her love and support.

With the odds against me succeeding in my own consultant firm being so great, that was quite a commitment from my angel. Time has proven that having faith and believing in God is rewarded. The lesson I learned is that with your hand in God's hand and with His blessings, all things are possible.

# Chapter 7

# My Career Role Models

I joined a small black CPA firm, King/Reynolds, which provided an opportunity to better utilize my accounting education and begin putting together the pieces of the financial puzzle. It was the village that raised me, but I now was faced with joining a small accounting firm to lead me in pursuing the vision and mission of my ultimate plan. I needed a new team of supporters and people who were interested in helping me and teaching me how to achieve my goals. I realized early in life that there are some things you don't learn in school.

Two CPAs, Mr. Benjamin L. King and Mr. Arthur M. Reynolds Sr., who were the role models for my career and professionalism aspirations. Mr. King was the first black CPA licensed in the state of Maryland, and Mr. Reynolds was one of the most brilliant men I had ever known. They took the time and had the patience to teach and prepare me for what was to come. They both initially worked as accountants and auditors for the federal government.

After graduating from HBCUs—Mr. King (Virginia State University) and Mr. Reynolds (Howard University)—they decided to do graduate study at American University to qualify them to sit for the CPA examination in Washington. Both chose AU because it was the first integrated university in the area.

When Mr. King decided to take the CPA exam, Washington required that he work for two years to qualify for the exam, and he could not find employment in any white-owned firms. He did find an established black accountant in Washington and went to him for employment.

The accountant told Mr. King that hiring him would launch a potential competitor, and he refused to hire him.

Mr. King said that he would never take that attitude and decided to help everybody who asked for his help. I knew then that he was the kind of leader I needed. Since Maryland did not have a work requirement, he and his family moved to Seat Pleasant, Maryland, and he took and passed the CPA exam.

As more black-owned businesses opened, Mr. King became the primary source for those who needed financial advice. Remember Mr. Payne and the village in chapter 2?

Mr. King taught accounting at Morgan State University and worked to have it recognized by the CPA board so the students could qualify for the state's CPA exam. Once they graduated, he made it a practice to hire the young accountants or help find them find work elsewhere. Mr. King eventually moved to Baltimore and opened a practice there. In 1973, he founded the Baltimore chapter of the National Association of Black Accountants and used it as a platform to help younger professionals learn and network. Can you see the similarities to the mission, vision, and founding of the Association of African American Financial Advisors (AAAA) presented in this book?

In his introduction speech, Mr. King impressed upon me that I was representing King/Reynolds when I was sent on an assignment. He said my dress and decorum must be impeccable, and I must be professional at all times. The partners would make sure I was prepared. Mr. King's always told me to "keep up the image at the line of scrimmage" because current and prospective clients would always be watching. He would often remind me that they would not accept anything but the best from me. Don't tell me that we don't have role models to follow.

Mr. Reynolds was teaching at Howard University and remained in Washington to service an accounting marketing base he had nurtured while he pursued a tax and business law degree from Georgetown University. A brilliant man, he was seemingly able to handle the most difficult tasks effortlessly. He had no problems passing the bar exam and started to make the transition from accounting to law. He continued to specialize in tax and business matters and was successful in his practice. He saw in me a somewhat raw talent and a hard worker who could be an asset to King/Reynolds. He must have gathered that I had a bright future ahead and did his best to help me along the way.

When Mr. King opened up an office in Baltimore, I became Mr. Reynolds's mentee and primary assistant. Even with his busy schedule, he had the patience to teach me and oversee my work and progress in the accounting firm. That is not a given in many professional firms; in their pursuit of profits, many devote very little time to training and developing employees. It was his motto that to be successful, you had to know how to work smart as well as hard.

In many cases, I was the one to service the firm's clients, and I became their primary contact for addressing their problems and concerns. The partners handled all technical issues and were liable for satisfying the needs of the clients. They signed all audit reports and tax returns and had all the face time in meeting with and acquiring new business. My job was a win-win proposition. The firm benefitted from my work, and I gained immeasurable experience, contacts, and exposure, which expedited my maturity and benefited me in my ultimate plan.

After Mr. King opened the Baltimore office, most of my career success, achievements, designations, and recognitions in the financial planning and advisory industry can be traced back to the tutoring and counseling of Mr. Reynolds. When an opportunity arose to host a business TV show at Howard University, they wanted him, but he recommended me for the *Common Cents* program. When an international contractor sought an economic and business specialist to service Bermuda, the Caribbean, and South America, they asked him first, but he recommended me.

When Mr. Reynolds decided to leave the accounting business and focus his attention on a budding tax and business legal career, he gave his accounting practice to me and recommended his clients to hire me since I had been doing most of their work anyway. To capitalize on the opportunities Mr. Reynolds provided me, I had to be prepared and ready to accept the opportunities and benefit from them. I was prepared and ready, and I welcomed them with open arms and God's blessings.

One of my first assignments for King/Reynolds put me in charge of the bookkeeping and accounting services for a nonprofit organization called United Communities Against Poverty (UCAP). During this assignment, I met the Honorable Judge Lucy B. Warr, then the executive director. I was encouraged and motivated by her and the mission and vision of UCAP. I saw the dedication and hard work they did to help the community and tend to the general welfare of others.

To perform my duties, I had to directly interact with Mrs. Warr. She appreciated the fact that I knew my assignment, but she offered valuable non-accounting advice that would help me in my professional development and career. She treated me like one of her sons and talked to me about the importance of proper appearance, decorum, and dress, which would benefit me later in life. She boosted my professional confidence, which allowed me to believe I could achieve success in my chosen career. She must have determined that I had followed her suggestions because she became one of my first clients when I began my own financial advisory firm.

Before her husband passed, he recommended that I handle her financial planning, tax, and consulting services if anything should happen to him. After his passing, she took his recommendation and retained me to be her personal tax accountant and financial advisor. I also provided these services to some of her children when they started their families and entered the work world.

I cherish and appreciate the patronage and guidance of Mrs. Warr for her contributions to my career. Her steadfast commitment to the welfare of the Prince George's community and her many other accomplishments as a public servant caught the attention of former Maryland governor Harry Hughes, and in 1984, he appointed her to the Prince George's County Orphan's Court. This appointment gave her the distinction of being the first African American female judge in the county. She became the chief judge in 1986, making her the first female chief judge in Maryland, and she served there until her retirement in 2001.

My other firm assignments and responsibilities were rendering tax and accounting services to many of the high-income African American professionals in the Washington area. These professionals were physicians, dentists, lawyers, federal and district government employees, businesspersons, and DC and Maryland government contractors. These clients represented nearly 90 percent of the accounts Mr. Reynolds gave me when he changed careers. These clients formed my projected marketing base when I began my solo accounting and financial planning practice.

The lack of foreseeable black business growth may have hastened Mr. Reynolds's career transfer to tax and business law. We were heading in the right direction, but he believed it would take a few years before he would see significant positive movement. Small accounting firms were primarily confined to bookkeeping and tax preparation, which were not considered high-profit centers. There were few tax planning and audit opportunities available to small firms. This situation has begun to change today as our assortment of businesses proliferated. We also began to patronize our black businesses and professional practices.

I saw my marketing base begin to grow, but it still needed additional incentives and changes in our behavior financial habits to truly make an impact on our economic and financial future. We still have a long way to go before recognizable progress is made. We have made tremendous advancement in our financial education, but that has not made an appreciable dent in our employment in the accounting and finance industries.

Large firms have hired a few African Americans, but there are too few if these numbers can be counted. Large firms have hired some, but if you can count the numbers, that means we are too few. Since the overwhelming majority of my marketing base was black, any future success began with the marketing base of the growth of black businesses and employment—and the resulting opportunities.

# Chapter 8

# Thanks for My Training and Exposure

---

Experiences have taught me that no matter what school you graduated from or the designations behind your name, to succeed, you must be given the opportunities and capitalize on them when they occur. I took a step back to reflect on several opportunities I was given and how they were two giant steps forward in my career as a financial planner and advisor.

My accounting and small business training and experience started with my employment with King/Reynolds and the tutelage of Mr. King and Mr. Reynolds. Because of my affiliation with Mr. Reynolds, Howard University selected me to be the host of a finance and economic television program called *Common Cents*. This program allowed me to interview noted financial specialists in federal and local government and in private industries. It gave me an opportunity to reach viewers who were interested in the program's focus, and they were an integral part of my ultimate plan.

I was able to assist brilliant future young up-and-coming black financial and investment experts, such as Randall Eley and Ed Brown, by giving them the public exposure they deserved. The program also allowed me to showcase the fact that we had competent black financial experts who were worthy of hiring and patronage. It gave me the impetus to start the Association of African American Financial Advisors to help our members participate and compete in the financial-services industry.

Other small business experience and training came from participating in the Small Business Administration (SBA) 8(a) Program. This federal government program was established to assist small minority businesses in acquiring federal government contracts. From this program, I learned the fundamentals of starting and operating a business and the administrative attention that must be present to be profitable and successful, including a business plan and working capital. Further, the program prepared me to deal with the various problems and trials small business often experienced, including lines of credit and the need for marketing skills and assistance. Many of the successful small businesses, like Social and Scientific Systems, were started with and benefited from this program.

I was a volunteer consultant to the DC Council's Committee on Economic Development, which was chaired by the Reverend James Coates. The committee's primary purpose was to develop methods to improve the economic development of the city's riot-torn corridors and improve the procurement and contract procedures employed by the DC government. This consultancy helped me establish contacts in the local government, which boded well for future business economic development opportunities with the city council and the mayor of DC.

The targeted businesses were in the restaurant, alcohol, entertainment, and cleaning and janitorial industries. Where would the working capital come from? Where were the essential bank lines of credit? Most of the cash flow came from the owners spending "tomorrow's money" and high-interest loans. The scarcity of necessary resources made it tough to survive and grow, and banks were reluctant to lend money to small businesses for fear of the nonpayment of the loans.

Another entrepreneurial opportunity was to contract with the DC government in the way the federal government operated the SBA's 8 (a) Program and set aside a percentage of contracts for small businesses. To allay some of the banks' fears of nonpayment, the DC program could guarantee the repayment to the banks since they could have insisted rights of overseeing the operations of those businesses with whom they contracted.

DC could also provide training and administrative help to the businesses by outsourcing some of those duties to accounting and legal companies that were part of the DC Plan. But since the federal government had oversight and authority of DC's budget, the obvious solutions to assisting small businesses and economic progress in DC had difficulty getting off the ground. I believe the federal government's concerns could have been mitigated and the DC Plan could have succeeded if not for politics.

Training and learning experience mean very little if you don't get the opportunity to apply them. In that regard, I was selected to the board of advisors for the Independence Federal Savings Bank, which was owned by black business owners and professionals. This experience helped me in my counseling assignments for the Bahamas Hotel and Allied Workers Union, the establishment of its savings bank, and the building and operation of an open-air market in Freeport.

A monumental step forward in my economic development and financial consulting business was my selection to the board of directors for Social and Scientific Systems (SSS). This company was a very important achievement in my career because of how and why the selection was made. The president of the company was an African American who was not satisfied with just achieving his personal success; he was determined to help other qualified and professional blacks to succeed also. SSS had no African Americans on the company's board, and the president pushed to change that.

Herbert J. Miller handpicked three African Americans for board positions, and I was one of them because of my finance, accounting, and business background. I was a member of that board for twenty-eight years. As a member of the board, I assisted in the conversion of his firm to an employee stock ownership company. SSS continued to grow in size and profitability, which required more experienced executive guidance. The chairman of the board was the president of a multibillion-dollar company, and he brought his leadership experience with him to SSS. Before Mr. Miller's death, he suggested that his family retain me as the financial advisor for his wife and the family trust.

Taking a step back, I recall the attitude of one of my role models. Mr. King promised he would help everyone he could as he climbed the ladder of success. Mr. Miller's decision was most impressive because that is what I would have done. He could have remained silent, sat back, and enjoyed the firm's success, but he didn't. In my board position, I interfaced with other members in making multimillion-dollar decisions, and I participated in approving many successful projects and proposals for the company.

With God's blessings and guidance, I was doing quite well in my endeavors, but something was missing in the pursuit of my ultimate plan. I took a step back and reflected on my true mission and goal to help and motivate others in handling their financial resources to support their families, enjoy life, and be wise stewards of God's blessings.

My first international business trip was to Brazil. This is a photo of Sugar Loaf (top) and Corcovado (bottom)

# Chapter 9

# AIFLD and International Exposure

My international exposure was not scripted, and it was quite unexpected. While I was an adjunct accounting professor at Howard University, one of my students was working as a top executive for the American Institute for Free Labor Development (AIFLD). Carvin Jefferson was searching for an economic development and financial specialist. He offered the job to Mr. Reynolds, but he respectfully declined because it did not fit his future plans. Mr. Reynolds suggested that he should talk to me. I never dreamed of taking a job dealing with international affairs.

I told Carvin I would consider the job if my first assignment was in Rio de Janeiro, but I was kidding when I made the request. To understand how absurd this request was, consider the fact that I was born and raised in a Washington ghetto with no travel experience and had barely ever left my village other than going to Wilberforce or going to summer camp in my youth. My only knowledge of Rio was from movies and books. I was partly swayed by its beaches and lifestyle. To my surprise Carvin took my request seriously and got his boss' approval, and I was faced with honoring my job acceptance.

God stepped in again and directed me to accept the job because it was part of his ultimate plan for me—and off to Rio I went. I was now the finance and economic development specialist for an organization with operations in Bermuda, the Caribbean, and South America. By the way, I spoke no Spanish or Portuguese and had to have an interpreter with me wherever I went.

AIFLD was affiliated with the AFL-CIO and was funded by United States foreign aid funds appropriated by Congress and from union dues money. It had an exemplary record of accountability as detailed in numerous government audits, including the General Accounting Office. AIFLD was often rumored to have accepted funds from the CIA, but that was proven untrue. This rumor may have contributed to my near-death experience (mentioned in chapter 1).

The institute's role was to provide trade union education, funds for social development projects, such as construction of homes for workers and vocational training, consulting help for accounting, and administrative overhead and office expenses. God promised he would never leave me, and He definitely was with me in my South American experience. He keeps His promises. He guided and protected me through many AIFLD trips and the dangers I encountered. I had assignments to many countries in South America Caribbean and Bermuda that had diplomatic relationship with the United States. AIFLD rendered many important services to strengthen and improve the operation of their unions.

I recall one assignment when I was helping a union in Quito, Ecuador. Carvin called me and told me to abort my assignment and report to Bogota, Colombia, immediately. When I inquired why and with whom I was to see, he said he could not tell me. When I asked about my specific assignment, I was told I would receive that information when I arrived. Not knowing my assignment, purpose, or who I was going to see, I refused to go to Bogota.

Carvin replied that the assignment came directly from the top man, and if I didn't go, "someone from the finance and accounting office had to go."

After I told Carvin that I still refused to go, he had to fly to Bogota instead. I never found out what the secrecy was about. I decided that if I could not take these types of assignments without questioning, maybe I was not the right man for the job. I returned to Washington, resigned, and decided to embark on establishing my own firm.

BHCAWU Pres. Thomas Bastian discussing the official opening of the Bahamas Workers' Cooperative Credit Union Complex with The Honorable Sir Lynden Pindling Prime Minister and Minister of Tourism. November 11, 1991

# Chapter 10

# The Bahamas

My AIFLD assignments included assisting the Bermuda Industrial Union, the Caribbean, and many South American unions in economic, financial, and administrative areas. My most memorable and lasting international economic and financial experience was in the Bahamas.

Though I worked on only two of its islands—Nassau and Freeport—I interacted with gracious and hospitable people on that beautiful set of islands. I spent most of my service time in Nassau working for and with the Bahamas Hotel Catering and Allied Workers Union (BHCAWU) to improve working conditions and fair compensation for its workers. Like many other Caribbean nations, the country's economy depended heavily on the tourism, hotel, and allied industries.

When I was an employee of AIFLD, a component of the AFL-CIO, I was sent to see how we could help the Bahamian workers who had already begun their union activities many years ago. I was instrumental in improving the BHCAWU's accounting and general business administration. Additional assistance was done in starting an economic development effort for the opening of a union-owned marketplace in Freeport, Grand Bahamas. With AIFLD's help, I worked with the union to build their headquarters and the Workers Bank building in Nassau.

In later years, BHCAWU contracted my company (LRD Management Group) to help them address the union's concerns with the various hazardous working conditions and critique how employers were addressing these issues. This was done by comparing the Bahamas union's plight and reasonable conclusions with American policies on dealing with similar issues. Although the Bahamas does not have comparable laws or regulations similar to those of the United States, I recommended positive steps to be put in place to protect and benefit the workers of the BHCAWU.

Because of my experience in helping the workers in cases such as these, I was at the top of the union's list of consultants and advisors to monitor and protect the workers' retirement benefits and pension investments. Trust and confidence are the rock of the financial-services industry, and I had gained them—as well as their belief that I would always do what was in the best interests of the workers.

I was selected to be the independent investment consultant for the Bahamas Hotel and Allied Industry Pension Fund (BHAIPF). Shortly thereafter, the Bahamas Hotel Industry Management Pension Fund (BHIMPF) selected me to accept the same position for them. For both organizations, I was the independent investment consultant for hundreds of millions of dollars and the welfare of the retirement investments for the hospitality and allied industries that represented 60 percent of the country's income and half of its employment.

My task was to monitor the investments status, investment managers' performance, and their adherence to the guidance and instructions of the respective boards' investment policy statements (IPS). I help design and adopt the IPS for both boards, determine the strategic target asset allocation included in the IPS for the US dollar and Bahamian dollar portfolios. I reviewed the annual reports from the Enrolled Actuary and Certified (Chartered) Public Accountants. I adopted the Bahamas, and they adopted me.

My Bahamian experience was one of the highlights of my financial advisory business because of its people and the importance of my services to them and their confidence in me. Can you imagine a small consulting firm monitoring and overseeing the performance of a multitrillion-dollar Wall Street investment company? I wondered how the investment managers of the pension funds would accept me looking over their shoulders, but they did so because the union workers and management pension boards required them to do so.

They elected to place their trust and confidence in me, which was generated from my years of service to the Bahamas, to assist the boards in carrying out their fiduciary responsibilities of protecting the pension funds' assets. My Bahamian experience fit perfectly into my mission, vision, and ultimate plan for helping those in need of my services— even if it was in a foreign land. It showed what can be done when we have trust and confidence in each other and when we are qualified and ready to take advantage of opportunities.

I had some difficulty explaining the importance of monitoring the transactions and cash flow of the pension fund assets to the board members. In my quarterly reports, I made frequent recommendations for them to ask their chartered accountants to include a random sampling of the assets that were in the hands of the custodian of each fund and to include comments in the audit management section of the annual audit reports. Some large brokerage houses have a subsidiary company acting as custodian of the fund assets, but if there is some disparity between the annual report and the periodic performance reports, they should look first to the custodian for clarity, reconciliation, and liability. The boards should clearly understand the role of the custodian and who to turn to for any liability claims.

I then received the boards' permission to have the investment managers include fees and compensation withdrawn from the account included in their periodic and annual performance reports. This data would allow me to show how they impacted the target portfolio returns, which were being withdrawn quarterly from the accounts in advance in my reports to the boards.

No investment management fees or compensation were billed to the pension funds. The important disclosure was to report investment manager performance before fees and compensation because performance can then better be compared to the benchmark and indices. This comparison would reveal the true value of the investment manager.

Further, I had each investment manager report their performance before and after fees and compensation withdrawals. These two examples illustrate the importance of the required guidance, reporting, and monitoring that should be presented in the IPS and to make sure the investment managers follow them. The boards of both pension funds were diligently trying to carry out their fiduciary responsibilities, address all investment activities, and take corrective actions when warranted. In most cases, they had the latitude and authority to make corrective management changes, but consultants are opinion givers and not decision makers. You can delegate authority, but you cannot delegate responsibility.

I learned a great deal from my Bahamas independent investment consultant assignment, and it prepared me for possible future institutional investment consulting endeavors. I thank the Bahamas for having the trust and confidence in me to be of service to them in undertaking this very important task of protecting the pension assets of the workers of the Bahamas.

# Chapter 11

# Becoming An Entrepreneur

After deciding to set up my own consulting firm, I had to determine my marketing base and develop my business plan. I had already reaped the benefit of the gifting of my accounting and tax clients from Mr. Arthur Reynolds, but that was only the beginning of a target market to reach my goals.

After some research and discussions with my initial clients, I found out about an African American social club known as Century Limited. Since African Americans could not join the segregated private white social club, a group of physicians, lawyers, and other professionals decided to form their own private club. The intent of the club was to have a place where African Americans could fellowship, have family gatherings, and keep members up-to-date with local politics and how they affected African American families.

The membership of this club was made up of some of the elite high-income professionals in the Washington, DC area. I felt that my membership in Century Limited would introduce me to potential clients for my financial advisory business and be a source for expanding my marketing base. I already knew some of the members from the list of clients I inherited from King/Reynolds, and they facilitated meeting and marketing my services to those I did not know.

Most of the members had graduated from Howard University Medical, Dental, or Law schools and other HBCUs. Some had graduated from prestigious white institutions, including Harvard, Georgetown, and American University. Many Century members held high-paying jobs in the federal government, which ultimately served to get me additional exposure and allowed me to expand my marketing base.

Although the members were high-income earners, they knew very little about financial planning and investing except for real estate, but they knew they had to pay income taxes. The fact that I had a tax background and had worked for King/Reynolds gave me the introduction I needed.

It didn't take long to increase my marketing base since Century's membership included the necessary DC and political contacts to get involved in the local economic development projects and commingle with influential social, business, and government leaders in the area. I was the only accounting and finance planning professional in the club, and I became the source members consulted when making tax and investment decisions.

This marketing strategy prepared me to advance from the initial operation of my economic and financial business and explore other business investments. In the midst of pursuing a career in the financial-services industry, I joined a group of prominent black DC businessmen to form Brookland

Enterprises Inc. (BE), which purchased real estate and ultimately opened a restaurant.

In Freeport, I helped establish a workers' bank and provided financing for housing and credit opportunities for union workers. Reflecting on this step back, I was able to take steps forward by using my Bahamas experience to provide financial guidance to BE in its real estate development entrepreneurial projects.

The other investors in BE included well-connected professionals: a lawyer, a real estate specialist, a dentist, a prominent restaurateur, and a retired professional football player. The real estate specialist, lawyer, and dentist were investors and founding members of the first black savings bank in Washington. BE felt that I brought the small business and economic development, accounting, financial expertise, and experience that was needed to succeed in our projected ventures.

We purchased a multifamily dwelling to begin our housing project, but we decided our dedication and devoted time were lacking. We decided to sell the multifamily dwelling and concentrate on building and operating a restaurant for elite and prominent Washingtonians, which was the dream of the company's restaurateur president. I felt the opening of an upscale restaurant with high-income patrons might result in clients for my financial-services firm, and the other stockholders of BE believed the restaurant would also benefit their businesses.

Choosing the right site to open the restaurant was our next assignment. We purchased a closed theater in northeast Washington with plenty of space and imagined the loyal customers of the president coming and bringing their families and friends. After meetings with architects and interior decorators, we were prepared to proceed with our restaurant.

BE had tried several economic projects but abandoned them in search of more profitable ventures. Some things you can plan for—and some you cannot. The death of several BE members contributed to inefficient succession planning changes and the direction of BE's business plan, which could have benefited us greatly and paved an easier road to success. We had no idea that an even better opportunity awaited us in a relatively short time: the establishment of a world-class restaurant that would become the meeting place for prominent clientele.

The key member for such a meeting place was our president. William Simpson brought a reputation from his famous steak house; his famous Ebony Table was the most sought after gathering place in Washington for blacks. The restaurant provided Washington's African American community with an upscale venue for dining and socializing in the period between segregation and Home Rule.

As soon as it opened, the restaurant became a popular meeting place for black intellectuals, professionals, politicians, and entertainers, as well as for African diplomats. African American Congressmen, journalists, and federal officials met regularly at the Ebony Table. In this forum, they discussed and strategized the political and civil rights events and activities of the day. Dining at the Ebony Table was by invitation only. What happened and was discussed at the Ebony Table stayed at the Ebony Table.

After Billy Simpson's death in 1975, *Washington Post* columnist William Raspberry wrote, "Hardly anything of significance in Washington—and most particularly to black Washington—came to fruition without Billy Simpson' significant—albeit non-public—role in it."

Billy Simpson's House of Seafood and Steaks was added to the DC Inventory of Historic Sites in 2008 and the National Register of Historic Places in 2009. At the funeral services, Monsignor Joshua Mundell said that Mr. Simpson was the city "unelected mayor" before Home Rule. He was definitely the one to lead BE in accomplishing his dream of a seafood restaurant on the Southwest Waterfront, but God had another plan.

The signing of the agreement between Brookland Enterprises, and the DC Redevelopment Agency to build the first African American restaurant on the Washington, DC Waterfront. The author is on second row, second person left.

# Chapter 12

# The Southwest Waterfront Saga

Washington had begun to plan for land leasing of severely underserved and deprived neighborhoods, which would displace many black residents, but they thought it would produce job opportunities and spur business growth. In deliberative sessions, the Mayor, the Redevelopment Land Agency (RLA), and the City Council began to discuss the possibility of how to approach the land leasing in ways that would ultimately benefit the people and improve the economic development of the city.

In the initial meetings, some council members cited that no blacks were being considered as possible lessees of any area that was predominantly black and balked at voting for the leasing plan. A dissenting councilman suggested that the council should at least be open to investigating the possibility of leasing some of the twenty-year, $8.5 billion-plan to blacks. According to a *Washington Post* article on January 14, 2004, this plan was to create new waterfront neighborhoods, parks, and amenities, rebuild roads and bridges, and build a sixteen-mile network of bicycle and walking trails along both sides of the Anacostia River and the adjacent Washington Channel.

The dissenting council members offered that residents and other Washingtonians were concerned about fair play and including blacks in the redevelopment of a predominately black city. After thorough investigation and deliberation, BE was awarded a ninety-nine-year lease of a parcel of land in the development plan, which was identified as the SW Waterfront. The mayor proposed, and the project was approved in 2004 by the city council by an 11–1 vote, the creation of a powerful corporation called Anacostia Waterfront Development Corporation. AWDC was charged with overseeing the development of the twenty-year project. The same *Washington Post* article noted that the AWDC appointed a seven-member board to execute the district's dramatic twenty-year plan.

The early development plans were easy compared to choosing a master developer and identifying the funding for such a large project. Years passed in the vetting and approving firms the city felt could qualify for the endeavor. That process got mired in political jockeying as to be expected. With a ninety-nine-year lease, BE felt that it should be given the opportunity to at least be included in the search and selection of the master developer.

BE hired a well-established law firm to represent us and began the search for a partner with development history and adequate resources and experience that we thought could meet the DC government's requirements. We did not expect to get a contract for the entire redevelopment of the twenty-year project; only the portion on which our ninety-nine-year lease was included, but we did not know how. Existing restaurants on the Waterfront received long-term leases and also had a vision of being a part of the new plan.

Any company chosen as the master developer had to contend with the businesses that had long-term leases. According to a *Washington Post* report from July 11, 2004, the plan required:

> "the coordinated efforts of powerful, turf-conscious agencies in both the city and federal governments, not to mention the enthusiasm and money of dozens of private developers. And ultimately the people of the United States also would have to approve, because the support of Congress is essential."

The chosen master developer had to put together a team with development experience, identifiable financial resources, and the proven ability to monitor and oversee the development. In retrospect, the death of our real estate specialist and attorney left a hole in our team's negotiation capabilities. Another contributing factor to our not being included in the developer's master plan was that our team did not replace the original members with adequate skills to meet the competition. After many years of posturing and lobbying by larger companies, BE was not selected as a participant in the selected master developer's plan.

The chosen developer's first choice for a development partnership withdrew because of the economy, the financial beating the real estate market was taking at the time, and the difficulty of identifying the necessary financial resources. Participation in this twenty-year, $8 billion saga was an experience of a lifetime for me and a small company like BE. Though we were not included in the master developer's plan or receive the financial reward we envisioned, with very tough negotiations, we still benefited financially. Had it not been for politics and being outmaneuvered by larger entities, the outcome could have been much different. We also had to take heed of the rumors of DC possibly taking over our lease via eminent domain to keep the development process going.

The government can acquire land through public use law, which applies to a use for property that is designed to benefit the public as a whole rather than just a private individual or entity. When a property the government is acquiring is from a private owner, the owner needs to be compensated. The compensation follows the guidelines in the Just Compensation in Eminent Domain law and is based on the value of the land the government is acquiring. In some cases, it includes the severance damage to the land they may be indirectly impacting.

The Just Compensation Clause in the Fifth Amendment states the following, "Nor shall private property be taken for public use, without just compensation." Just compensation is fair-market value of a parcel of property that must be paid to a landowner who has had their property taken by the government.[1]

After tense and complex negotiations and possible legal costs to pursue the matter, BE decided to settle for an amount

---

[1] "Just Compensation in Eminent Domain," Biersdorf & Associates.

less than we wanted—but it may have been more than just compensation as determined by the courts.

Whenever I'm in the Southwest Waterfront area or read about its development, I reminisce about what could have been. It reminds me of the history of black people who own tremendously valuable land in many parts of the United States that is now—after many years of redevelopment and regentrification—worth millions of dollars. In hindsight, we can question the decisions that we had to make back then, but one needs to appreciate the times when those decisions were made. Today, there is no difference. There has been much improvement in that regard, but some vestiges of those occurrences still exist today.

# Chapter 13

# Entering the Financial Planning Industry

When I decided on a financial planning career, I made it my goal to be the best financial planner I could be. Financial planning was exactly in harmony with the mission and vision of my ultimate plan. I just had to step back, remember those goals and objectives, and stay focused while I learned.

After extensive research of new ways to accomplish my goals, I discovered the emergence of a new profession called financial planning, which included concepts and process that were closer to my mission and goals and objectives better than my previous focus on accounting and income taxes. I saw articles of this relatively new profession of an organization called the International Association of Financial Planners (IAFP), the predecessor organization to the Financial Planning Association (FPA).

The association's mission, purpose, and holistic approach to solving personal financial problems were compatible with mine. To find out more about FPA, I attended several meetings of the local chapter: the National Capital Area (NCA). I saw no members who looked like me and was curious as to why. After much thought, anxiety, and consternation, I decided to join and participate in the financial planning movement, which I thought could help me accomplish my mission.

When I joined the IAFP, I wanted to learn as much as I could about financial planning and participate in the movement in the best way I could. I took on committee assignments and joined roundtable discussions concerning the industry—and I evidently impressed other members who thought I had leadership capabilities.

My journey was not easy, and many times, only divine intervention carried me through some tenuous situations. However, I only had a few touchy experiences during my early NCA membership days. In fact, I developed friendships with several members who welcomed me and offered encouragement and help. However, for many NCA members, it was a case of benign neglect. Very few considered me competition since their marketing base strategy did not include African Americans, and they did not think I could penetrate their base.

I could not count on others to help me achieve the goals and mission of my ultimate plan. I felt then and now that the African American population was a fertile ground for starting and building a profitable financial planning and advisory practice. They knew very little about financial planning, and I had to reach them to teach them. Once they knew the industry, they would seek financial services and consultation.

Hosting the Howard University's *Common Cents* program gave me excellent exposure and interaction with the program's expert guests and panelists, which resulted in additional benefits for me. I realized that the clients Mr. Reynolds gave me were primarily Howard University's professionals, and they were also ardent viewers and supporters of the *Common Cents* program.

I had a good client retention rate because of the care and personal attention required by my marketing base and growing small business community, which ended up being a good marketing referral source. I kept in contact with the client families' children and other family members who noticed how well I handled their parents and relatives, and upon the death of family members, they became clients. I have enjoyed the patronage of some of my clients for more than forty years. The best advertisement for my services was its book of satisfied clients.

# Chapter 14

# The First Black Certified Financial Planner

Though my peers and oversight associations always thought it to be, Wall Street, banking, insurance industries, and finance moguls hesitated to embrace the Certified Financial Planner (CFP®) designation as the gold standard for financial planning. I took a step back, remembered the mission and goals of my ultimate plan, and began the pursuit of my CFP® designation by enrolling in the College for Financial Planning in Denver, Colorado.

Studying and learning from members in my IAFP-NCA chapter, I successfully completed my studies and received my CFP® designation on November 3, 1978, at the ninth conference and conferment of the school, becoming the first African American in the country to do so. The college was founded in 1972 as the primary educational source for the CFP® designation since the industry was in its infancy stage. Passing the exam and obtaining the designation was one thing, but how would I use it to pursue my mission and have a successful financial planning career?

Being the first black to receive the CFP® designation resulted in many interviews, publications, awards, and overall exposure, which led to my true introduction to the financial-services industry. I was able to leverage the designations to the fullest and take advantage of every opportunity presented to me. My goal was to bring other African American financial planners along with me and be a part of the solution to vastly improve the economic condition of our people. In so doing, we could mitigate the degradation of our communities and the fallout resulting from crime, home foreclosures, and disharmony in our families in the rearing of our children.

I wanted to motivate our people to know and believe that what God did for me, He will do for them if they just open the door to their hearts and let Him in. I believe that financial literacy is the key. Teaching personal finance should begin in elementary and middle schools so the proper learning foundation of handling finance and debt management and saving and investing can be put on solid ground as children approach adulthood.

I was a member of a group that attended a Maryland House session to support legislation making financial literacy a part of the curriculum for elementary schools. A very high-level state official who tried to get the legislation through the House for some time supported this effort. When ask to pass this legislation, one of the representatives replied that financial literacy should be taught in the homes and not mandated by politicians. How could the children who most needed financial literacy get the proper teaching of it in homes where the parents needed help in this regard as much as the children did? Such legislation would have gone a long way toward getting the attention of African Americans, and it could have been a motivating force in improving our communities.

If I could provide some impetus to mitigate this social and economic ill, I would take giant steps forward in my ultimate plan. If I could use my achievements in the financial planning industry as an example to excite, motivate, and encourage our youths and families of the importance and benefits of financial planning, it could greatly improve the chance of bettering our communities. The benefits of financial planning are applicable to all—regardless of income, education, or career.

Alexandra Armstrong CFP® providing assistance
and guidance to me on the right.

# Chapter 15

# Help Is on the Way

My first financial planning mentor is truly responsible for whatever success I've achieved in the industry. I met Alexandra Armstrong at an FPA/NCA meeting. This wonderful young lady was a financial planning pioneer in her own right, having been the first person to earn the Certified Financial Planning certification CFP® in Washington, DC. She later became a noted author, having coauthored *On Your Own: A Widow's Passage to Emotional and Financial Well-Being*. She was pushing for diversity & inclusion for women in the financial planning industry before it became popular. She encouraged and mentored me during my earlier years in the FPA/NCA. When she was serving as the president, I was on several committees under her leadership. After completing her tenure, she recommended me for the presidency.

At the time, I was still the only African American I saw at meetings and national conferences. At a national symposium, she saw me standing alone and not mingling or talking to other attendees and staring like a deer in headlights. She came over to welcome me to the conference and suggested to always enter a room like you belong there. She said someone is always watching—and I must show an air of confidence in myself to make it in the financial planning industry. I believe her support and efforts to encourage me forward and upward in FPA/NCA were not very popular among some of the other chapter members.

I was elected president of the FPA/NCA and became, I believe, the first African American president of an FPA/NCA chapter. I believe she was responsible for my election. Her support and guidance did not stop there. She definitely had a hand in my selection for the FPA/NCA 2008 Lifetime Achievement Award. At my acceptance of the award, I said thanks to her by publicly acknowledging her leadership in championing diversity in the industry and extending her hand to me in friendship and offering me help when I needed it. I called her my Good Samaritan because, as others passed me by, she offered help and provided me support in my entry into the financial planning industry.

When I decided to do my part in pushing for diversity & inclusion in the industry, I determined that the movement must include African Americans, and there was a lot of ground to cover. To meet the task, I founded the Association of African American Advisors to help our advisors gain valuable exposure, obtain clients, and pass on the success of a few of us to the next generation. Alex was one of the first contributors to the AAAA. I founded the 501(c)(3) organization to prepare members for participation and representation in the financial advisory industry.

Dr. Robert N. Ginsburgh gave me important counseling after I received my Certified Financial Planning certificate from the College for Financial Planning. He invited me to lunch at a prestigious membership club in Washington. Dr. Ginsburgh, a retired air force general and Harvard PhD, was on the National Security Council staff during the Johnson administration. He was editor-in-chief of *Strategic Review* and chairman of his financial planning and portfolio management firm. He also taught courses in economics, international relations, personal finance, and insurance at West Point. I mention his credentials and positions to highlight my amazement that he saw enough promise in me to offer his unpaid counseling and congratulations for my receiving the CFP® designation.

When I arrived early for the lunch, the doorman thought I was at the wrong place because blacks were not usually seen at the club. When Dr. Ginsburgh arrived, he was incensed but not surprised and let the management know it. His purpose for the meeting, as he put it, was to impress on me that "passing the exam may get me to the table," but he wanted to give me some advice on "how to get something off the table." He suggested the first step of establishing a marketing base for my practice and focusing on acquiring and servicing them, building on that base, and always being a student of my profession. He said that a good financial planner should have an opinion about any subject affecting their clientele and to be able to substantiate the opinions by doing their research and study "homework."

Time management is of major importance, especially for independent financial advisors, so you must concentrate on being on top of your market base first and other issues to follows. Chasing the high-income market when the odds of obtaining those clients may not be good time management for the beginner and small financial advisors. If most of your marketing base has a conservative or moderately conservative investor profile, would their marketing base be attracted to alternative investments?

Even if I chose to work for a brokerage or investment firm, I would be like a small company operating as a subsidiary of a parent company—and I would still have to produce to succeed. Developing my marketing base would continue to be my first concern. I needed to create my own business plan, develop prospects, and provide the personal attention and advice they needed.

Alexandra Armstrong and Dr. Robert Ginsburgh motivated me and laid the groundwork for my practice and financial planning career. They told me that you never know who is watching and to always look and act professionally and be prepared to take advantage of opportunities when they come. Only God could have sent the help of these two individuals when I really needed help in starting my financial planning career.

# Chapter 16

# Starting My First Financial Planning Company

To extend my financial education and continue to reach forward in my ultimate plan, I decided to start a firm dedicated to the financial planning and advisory principles compatible with my mission and vision. With the help of my friend Charles Norris, I formed LeCount R. Davis & Associates. As an insurance representative, Charles brought that expertise to the table.

To provide effective and comprehensive financial advice, we knew several professions and expertise were needed. The associates were not employees, but they were vetted and had to meet our criteria in terms of education, licenses, and designations. They were lawyers, tax accountants, insurance representatives, stockbrokers, and real estate specialists. This was my original team, and the dance continued two steps forward.

There is a big difference between being an employee of supporting, sheltering, and knowledgeable bosses and operating an independent practice. There were financial and human resources to be considered: a business plan, working capital, office expenses, and hiring and training employees. Success or failure could be determined by client marketing skills and developing a client base to support my business plan.

I would always ask myself a question: If I were in a room of prospective clients, what would make them choose you as their financial planner and/or financial advisor? I did not think too many of my peers had any international experience or exposure to a target market in a foreign land. I was an IRS-enrolled agent, which permitted me to represent clients before the IRS and my enthusiasm and desire to professionally represent and serve my clients would be evident and exemplary. Trust and confidence are the bedrock of financial planning and advisory service. I insisted that my team members, including myself, exude outstanding trust qualities—and their competence, licenses, and achievements would meet the highest standards.

Things were a little tough back then, mainly because of the lack of working capital. A line of credit was not available for minority startup businesses with marginal balance sheet numbers. The team never took the vital step of sharing common operational costs: office rent, administrative help, and research and development. Thanks to Jewel, we had our family budget well in focus, which allowed me to meet my initial expenses. With God's blessings, I survived and moved onward and upward.

My initial plans had certain difficulties from the start. I failed to recognize that team members had certain restrictions for which affiliations they could and could not have. Since I was a fee-only planner and advisor, I had to disclose any "soft benefits" from anyone, which is something that some of the associate advisors did not want to do.

Eventually, I had to change plans and team members. This independent team approach is highly touted today—for startup and small advisors—as the best way to compete in the financial-services industry. If the team members are not selling the same service of products, competition should not be a problem. Many financial advisors did not believe one could succeed as a fee-only financial planner, but time has proven them wrong.

The industry was built on commission compensation, but with the changes in political legislation and industry regulations, times have changed, which also caused advisors to change how they practiced. The new regulations did not dictate how financial advisors practice, but they do require more transparency and reasonable compensation disclosure to protect investors and provide them a chance to make decisions that put the investors first when choosing investments. These are the principles my financial practice have always honored, but it took President Obama's legislation—insistent requirement of the fiduciary rule—to hold advisors to change the old way of doing things.

A Dallas court determined that the fiduciary rule overstepped its authority and allowed for President Trump's retreat from the purpose of the rule to help investors. However, some companies decided that the rule was just and placing the industry to be liable was warranted. Many industries have balked at being proponents of the rule since the court's decision. No objective professional opinion should find fault with the rule.

The industry was based on commission compensation and the liability of the advisor as the justification for the political decision to repeal the legislation. Many brokers and bankers decided that they needed those perks to maintain their standard of living and escape liability when caught operating in ways that did not put the investor first and not having to adhere to full transparency and compensation disclosure. There is a fiduciary rule that states you can delegate authority—but you cannot delegate responsibility.

My reflections on the problems of black entrepreneurship brought to mind a manuscript I wrote and sent to Spike Lee in hopes that he would make it into a movie to focus on the problems we had in starting and operating businesses. The title of that book was *One Step Forward and Two Steps Back*. Spike Lee politely replied that he only produced movies for stories he wrote.

The moral of that story was the steps our people took to open and profitably operate and patronize each other because we didn't have many options to do otherwise. As more options became available, we took two steps back and reduced or eliminated purchasing goods and services from our own people. Many of our people produced comparable products and rendered excellent services. It is ironic that we spend large dollars to provide our children a top-rated education but never give any thought to who will be their employers, clients, or customers. That situation exists today.

We will not do business with each other. We think in short-term and selfish ways: What is cheaper for us and not our people? We could create our own mini economy to support us and our communities and create jobs for our people. I understand the rationale created by myths and the search for profitability. However, I also believe that there will be no substantial economic improvement for African Americans until we find ways to help others while we are doing well ourselves.

That philosophy motivated me to seek entrepreneurship for myself. As Mr. Reynolds taught me, the only way to earn a living is money at work or people at work. Since I had little money to work for me, I started a business while helping others. I have not worked for any company or organization for more than forty years and decided to do it my way. I refused to be boxed in and be what others wanted me to be. It wasn't always easy, but that's what walking by faith is all about.

# Chapter 17

# Developing a Strategic Plan

I took a step back in history to recall what my people had to deal with, their trials and tribulations, and what they had to overcome to take financial and economic steps forward. I recalled God's divine intervention and blessings throughout my people's history. It seemed to bring into perspective how relatively small a challenge I had to face to succeed. I still marvel at the fact that my father was raising a family while having periodic employment and less than normal poverty wages. We didn't even know we were poor because we never lacked food, clothing, or shelter. My family and village's knowledge of money and finance was limited at best, and in most cases, it was nonexistent. In my research, I found out that a few of us managed to survive, support our families, and accumulate some wealth despite the challenges.

I was impressed by the accomplishments of "Black Wall Street" in Greenwood, Oklahoma, which was described by many as the epicenter of African American entrepreneurship and wealth in the early twentieth century, before its destruction. Reginald Lewis was a successful black Harvard University graduate and multimillionaire who authored *Why Should White Boys Have All the Fun?* We had many successful business owners in our history who could serve as our role models if we would take the time to learn our history. Our stories are rarely taught in white schools, so we have to intensify our efforts to learn our history.

There are two ways to earn money: people at work (entrepreneurship) and money at work (saving and investing). I sought to find ways to save and invest to accumulate money, grow the wealth of our masses, provide for the distribution of the wealth to improve our communities, and transfer that wealth to future generations by saving and investing. Embedded in the growth of wealth should be learning how to spend wisely, provide for our families, and be faithful stewards of God's blessings.

Taking a step back, I recalled Dr. Ginsburgh's advice of determining a marketing base to start my financial practice and build on it as you find and service other clients. A sound foundation of a practice is essential when starting a financial planning practice. He further impressed on me that if you set future goals too high, you may become frustrated and adopt a "loser" attitude when you don't reach those goals.

Several African American financial advisors fell into that trap and never recovered. They would go from one firm to another, never satisfying the blind optimism goals required by the "book" mentality of the brokerage houses, banks, and insurance companies. They were not financial planners; they were salesmen of financial products. I chose not to take that route and sought a different road to travel.

I knew I had to put extra efforts into reaching and teaching my people the proper way to spend, save, and invest. In order to teach them, I had to reach them—and focusing on our financial behaviors and money attitudes was a good place to start. The basic principles of financial planning and its virtues was a good next step. Many African Americans don't know what financial planning is; therefore, they cannot begin to value its benefits. Until that is done, they will not be, in great numbers, participants in the financial planning process. An intentional and concentrated effort to reach African Americans had to be made to develop and promote financial literacy programs to reach them in all age groups and all income categories.

Knowing that we looked at a lot of television, we see mostly negative media stories about criminal activities, entertainment shows, and sporting events because that is how the stations make money. I know that, but the information our people need to better themselves and communities are not present. Taking a step back, I recall a time when I went to the office of the president of a TV owner whose programs targeted blacks to ask that information on how we handle our finances could be a valuable tool in improving our communities.

He said, "Black people do not know anything about money."

I replied, "That is the reason you could help our people by airing such information."

My argument was not saleable, and we continue to make money off our people, but we do very little to improve the financial conditions of our people and communities.

An exception to that scenario was Howard University's public broadcasting station. The WHMM program *Common Cents* was produced to do just that. Its purpose was to educate our people on how to deal with their finances and how that can teach, influence, and motivate black people to take steps to improve their financial stewardship—and thus help ourselves and our communities. Further, the program introduced other black professionals who were involved in economics and finance to inform others that we had capabilities to help them better themselves and our communities.

I began my financial literacy project by publishing a newsletter "Finance and the African American Family," and I began giving seminars at churches, black Greek letter organizations, and black professional groups. The newsletter was received well, and I was able to, as a side benefit, receive many requests for my services. Since a satisfied client is your best advertisement, each referral had a surprising compounding effect on the growth of my practice.

I believe African American advisors need to intensify their marketing efforts by replicating this proven strategy, which includes helping our communities and acquiring new business, especially churches, social groups, senior citizens, and various age groups whose main purpose is to better the financial and economic status of our people and Greek letter organizations. African Americans are making much more money and have better-paying jobs than ever, but we are also spending more. It's not how much you make; it is how much you retain that's most important. Watch the progress of your net worth and do not focus solely on how much you earn. That should be your motto. Closely monitor your discretionary spending.

Proceeding further in that direction, I was able to convince my church that financial literacy was vitally needed in our communities, and I became the chair of Mt. Calvary Baptist Church of Rockville, Maryland. The purpose and emphasis of Family Financial Literacy Ministry (FFLM) was on financial education. I brought in well-credentialed black specialists in the various financial professional areas I thought the church needed to know more about. This was done to give exposure to well-qualified, educated, and experienced black financial professionals.

I believe every church serving the black communities should have a FFLM. I further believe every organization that supports and promotes bettering the lives of black people should put financial literacy in our communities near the top of their agendas and be intentional about it. For an example of the impact of financial literacy, I need only step back and look at what it has accomplished—and is still doing—in the lives of two FFLM representatives.

Since I believe financial literacy should be a family affair, I chose the Howard and Sherrell Nicholson family as the first family representative of FFLM. The family attended and participated in the presentation of FFLM events. Over the years, the Nicholson parents have sought advice from financial professionals they connected with at FFLM events to help plan for their family financial needs as they've evolved—from overall family financial planning to retirement and estate planning. I was pleased to learn that the Nicholsons' daughter Kyra, a recent medical school graduate, asked her parents to assist her in identifying a financial planner to help her start her medical career on sound financial footing. The Nicholson family has begun helping their eldest son, Howard III, a college senior and outstanding student destined for a brilliant career in the field of biomedicine, build a foundation of fiscal responsibility and discipline.

For the Nicholson children, it was their faith and belief in God, instilled in them by their parents and church family, that directed their paths and helped sustain them. The second family representative of FFLM was the Jeffrey and Myra Byrd family. They also have a success story to tell. Their oldest daughter, Dr. Morgan Byrd, has already begun her career in physical therapy. Their oldest son, Jeffrey Colin, is a graduate of Morehouse College in Atlanta, and he is a third-year medical student at Morehouse School of Medicine and is pursuing a career as an orthopedic surgeon.

Drew, the youngest son, is a brilliant student at Morehouse College and has a double major in Chinese and Economics. As a part of the Career Leadership Institute at Morehouse College, Drew and twelve other Morehouse students visited various Fortune 500 companies on Wall Street, including Goldman Sachs, Bloomberg, CIT, Moody's, NBC Universal, and J. P. Morgan, to acclimate them to how Wall Street and major financial companies function. This opportunity also established strong business relationships and prepared students who are interested in finance, business, and media employment.

The youngest daughter, Logan, is following in the footsteps of her parents and siblings as an overachiever. She is destined for a successful professional ballet career. Logan is currently a conservatory student at City Dance School and Conservatory in North Bethesda, Maryland. Logan has also attended summer intensives with the School of American Ballet in New York City, the Pacific Northwest Ballet in Seattle, the Dance Theatre in Harlem, Koresh, and others.

The 1st family representative of Mt. Calvary FFLM

FFLM's success in motivating our families and youth could greatly benefit the future of our families and communities. When I step back and reflect on these two stories, I realize they are consistent with and meet the mission and vision of my ultimate plan.

I was a fee-only financial advisor and did not sell any financial or insurance products. While I did the vetting of all presenters at our seminars and workshops, I primarily moderated the events and made sure that presenters did not market the attendees at the church's seminars. The church made the proper disclosure that it was qualified to provide financial and tax advice and that the programs were for educational purposes only. Attendees were advised to seek advice from a personal financial or tax advisor before attempting to implement any recommendations.

The presenters could pass out their cards, and if attendees wished to retain them after the seminars, they could. I personally insisted that attendees should know how to select a qualified professional financial planner or advisor who was properly licensed and regulated by some authority and/or the federal or state government.

Without any efforts, other churches began to hear about FFLM and became interested in setting up a similar program to financially educate their congregations and communities. Many of the financial specialists—lawyers, financial planners, brokers, and insurance representatives—did acquire clients from participating in the seminars. I also brought in government officials and organizations that supported financial literacy to explain how to go about taking action against those who sought to take advantage of attendees through scams or misinformation.

Many organizations have been promoting financial literacy as a way to benefit our communities and improve our financial behaviors and habits. The AAAA Foundation and the Society for Financial Education & Professional Development (SFE&PD), headed by Ted Daniels have put financial literacy at the forefront of their agenda. In 2018, I was honored and privileged to receive SFE&PD's highest award (Eagle) for my leadership in financial planning and strong commitment to financial literacy. I proudly include this award in the list of awards at the end of this book.

There is a big difference between our historical financial behavior and our current financial behavior. We have come a long way in improving our financial behavior, but we still have a long way to go. We are earning more and accumulating more wealth, but we still need directions for improving our saving, investing, and spending habits. The black population's buying power is continuing to grow, which may be good for the economy, but it could also increase our spending and slow good savings and investing habits.

Too much money and the lack of money corrupt, destroy families and communities, and increase criminal activities in our communities. I felt this was an opportunity to develop a platform for a successful practice that would fit my ultimate plan. However, that is easier said than done, especially when you stay in survival mode for too long. My strategic plan took some time to implement, and I had to hold on until my practice produced enough revenue to cover my practice's expenses, provide support for my family, and reach my projected profitability level. With God's blessing and my wife's cooperation and support, I was successful in doing that.

I noticed that African American financial planners and advisors stayed in survival mode for too long—due to no fault of their choosing. Many were jumping from one firm to another in search of the right mix, but they still had to produce revenue for their employers and firms. Their plans depends on the firm's plans that required certain adjustments to deal with.

Brokerage representatives were mainly salesmen and not planners or advisors, and the financial products and services they sold dictated their companies' primary plans. The clients' interests were not always consistent with the products and services sold; they were based on the commissions that could be earned. I understood that, and I knew that was not the way I wanted to operate.

The financial-services industry is constantly changing, and it requires us to adjust to the changes. The larger financial-services institutions have embraced the affiliation with independent advisors and face greater regulatory demands for better compensation transparency, which required them to make some changes. There has also been a movement toward robo advisory services. I did not think that my marketing base, as well as the general public, would be eager to go from no investment participation to taking advice from machines and technology. They prefer a personal, face-to-face relationship with their advisors.

The financial-services industry has begun to recognize that African Americans have become more sophisticated and are increasingly seeking financial advisors who look like them, are trustworthy, and have their best interests at heart.

Lazetta Rainey Braxton, MBA, CFP® Board Chair
of AAAA and President of AAAA Foundation.
She is one of the leaders in the financial planning
industry Diversity & Inclusion movement

# Chapter 18

# Association of African American Financial Advisors

I practiced as a fee-only CFP® and observed the positives and negatives of an African American operating and surviving in the financial-services industry. I was able to determine substantial roadblocks for us to build our practices and take our rightful and well-earned place in the industry.

The education level of financial planning has taken giant steps forward. The number of African American Certified Financial Planners began to grow (way too slowly), and the industry had begun to recognize our presence. The numbers were few, and we had difficulties improving the profitability of our practices. We had to improve our brand, visibility, and exposure to attract clients because referrals were few at best and primarily nonexistent for most of us. I saw a need for African American financial planners and advisors to unite in our efforts to improve our future as the industry finally began to improve its diversity & inclusion outreach.

In 2001, I founded the Association of African American Financial Advisors (Quad A). I recruited eighteen highly qualified individuals who committed their time, energy, and resources to move the association forward. My new firm, LRD Management Group, provided the startup capital to cover the initial costs of the association. We received our 501(c) 3, tax-exempt status, which enhanced our funding opportunities.

The association's mission is to provide a forum for the professional development, training, and visibility of its members. Our goal is to build a membership of African American financial advisors who are highly qualified and recognized as leaders in the financial advisory industry. It is also our goal to be an effective network that will remain on the cutting edge of the financial advisory industry in order to enable members to be more competitive in providing financial and economic consulting services to the underrepresented as well as those of the middle- and high-income brackets.

We began as a local association focusing on the Washington, DC area, but as planned, we sought to become an independent organization that covered the entire country. We knew the road would be rough and the going would be tough and that we would need strong and committed members and leadership.

Special kudos goes out to Lanta Evans-Motte, a member of the first Quad A board. Her tireless dedication to our mission, administrative skills, and recruiting contributed heavily to the growth and success of Quad A. She later became president and joined with Tyson Bellamy (subsequent Quad A president) in procuring and servicing a contract with Montgomery County, Maryland, to provide financial counseling to its citizens.

After treading water while building the leadership base and attaining the notoriety we coveted, we had to move on to accomplish our mission and realize our vision. We did exceptional pro bono work for the communities we serve and promoted financial literacy programs throughout Washington, Maryland, and Virginia. We welcomed young and aspiring black advisors to join us in seeing that financial planning and advice was needed by all—throughout the country—but we needed to pick up the pace and do more.

One of those young, intelligent, resourceful, and energetic financial planners was Lazetta Rainey Braxton. She came to Quad A with impeccable education and experience credentials. She holds a BS degree in finance and international business from the University of Virginia and an MBA in finance and entrepreneurship from Wake Forest University. Lazetta has spoken on financial planning topics for national audiences and been featured in national publications. The fee-only RIA company she founded, Financial Fountains, provided services to all, including middle-income, mass-affluent, and underrepresented markets. The reigning president of Quad A, Crystal Alford Cooper, recruited her.

After some consideration and thought, she decided to join Quad A. She jumped in with both feet, became president of Quad A, and subscribed to all that national membership and recognition would be our goal. After seeing her presented with a 2015 *InvestmentNews* Women to Watch recipient, I knew we had found the right person to lead Quad A in our mission to receive national recognition.

With outstanding leadership, commitment, hard work, and substantial sponsorship resources, AAAA achieved its milestone presence with our first national conference in Boston in 2015. We followed that initial national conference with one in Baltimore (2016), one in Chicago (2017) and one in Atlanta (2018). Kudos to our past and present leadership who have given so much of themselves to build, engender hope, and provide guidance to so many. To an organization that has been through the fire and the rain, it was God's grace that brought us thus far. In God, there is always hope.

Some companies have embarked on an intensive program to create diversity & inclusion in their future plans to take advantage of a changing profitable workforce. If large companies and other organizations are really sincere in their efforts to promote diversity & inclusion, they should partner with organizations like AAAA. They could outsource certain functions: researching, identifying employment candidates, and training new employees who would fit into their future plans. In so doing, they could benefit from the increased participation of African Americans in the financial advisory industry.

We also could assist them in filling the gap caused by financial advisors who are retiring or leaving the business by hiring and introducing us to the requirements expected by the industry. Some surveys have projected that African American spending power will be in excess of $1.2 trillion by 2020, and it is growing. If the right kind of partnering is developed to allocate a fraction of this spending power to saving and investing, all participating partners would benefit. Certainly, such optimistic possibilities should be explored. AAAA is poised and prepared to take the leadership in making any partnering between African Americans and the financial advisory industry a success.

AAAA Foundation

The goal of the foundation is to develop a pipeline of African American financial planners and advisors, educate them, and give them the necessary visibility and exposure to succeed and become the best they can be in the financial-services industry. I joined my AAAA members in setting up the AAAA Foundation to address those issues and intensify our efforts to serve our communities and those who can't afford our services. I believe that the more you give, the more you receive.

The foundation realized that we must first create a strategy to convince African Americans that the financial planning and advisory profession is worthy of their attention and that it could provide an outstanding opportunity to participate in a complex and growing economic environment. In so doing, African American advisors could cultivate a marketing program for African American advisors that would contribute to their own financial plan while providing valuable services to our communities.

However, I wanted our foundation to pursue further steps that I thought fit in my ultimate plan: helping our communities and others in need. This required more pro bono work and increased financial literacy focus. Repetition can be a powerful tool to those who need counseling. To help our communities, we realize that most families need to earn enough money to provide for food, clothing, shelter, and health care. That is the only way to economically survive and prosper.

Financial literacy is the key, and it was a part of my ultimate plan. The more African Americans know of financial planning, the more they will participate in the process. We will begin to see the benefits of setting financial goals and objectives, spending wisely, saving, and investing. We will begin to learn how to transfer our wealth accumulation to future generations and help others in need through our charitable giving.

To begin our rescue efforts, we decided to increase our planning and advisory pipeline by focusing on HCBUs to provide the necessary guidance needed. I think they have the compassion, knowledge, and desire to help our people better themselves and our communities. Those of us currently in the industry could become role models for the next generation of financial advisors and an inspiration to the population and communities we serve.

I received congratulation for being selected for Investment News's 2018 Lifetime Achievement Award. Lazetta Rainey Braxton was awarded one of the See it Be it Role Model

# Chapter 19

# Diversity & Inclusion

---

Solving the diversity & inclusion problem is a very complex and difficult endeavor. You must first describe diversity & inclusion and realize their problems before you can come up with a viable solution. Diversity (D) is the blending of different backgrounds, experiences, and perspectives to infiltrate the workforce or necessary affiliations if employment is not the objective. Inclusion (I) involves having a seat at the table and being intimately involved in decision-making in a collaborative environment that welcomes meaningful participation from individuals and different ideas and perspectives that have positive impacts on business.

Diversity efforts have been talked about for years with little success in the hiring of the underserved African American population. On the other hand, inclusion has been elusive in the financial-services industry and is difficult to embrace. In realizing this, I wanted to see African Americans considered in the inclusion efforts being espoused and talked about by the financial-services industry.

The excuse for not being included in the diversity & inclusion discussions used to be the lack of financial education required by the industry. We have made tremendous strides in that regard, but the industry is now promoting that we do not have the necessary experience to benefit the industry. Further the myth is that if the D&I movement was promoted and implemented, it would result in inefficiency and a reduction of company profits. Numerous surveys and research have proven that has not been the case.

How do you get the experience if you are not hired or affiliated with industry leaders? Many investment and brokerage firms have established "book" minimums that preclude them from hiring employees. I believe the industry should approach diversity & inclusion in the same way they plan for launching a new product and/or service: with a long-term strategy. It takes time for a new product to fulfill its destiny, and the same should be expected when embarking on a serious diversity & inclusion project.

African Americans who have the proper education, credentials, and licenses should be given the opportunity to prove their worth over time. When the industry requires African American aspirants to have a minimum wire-house book of business exceeding millions of dollars, they immediately eliminate practically all African Americans. In pursuing an effective D&I program, the financial services must realize that we are not playing on a level competitive field and must allow for some beginning adjustments.

I knew the book issue would be difficult to satisfy since most African American advisors would have a marketing base of first-generation money who had not been planners, savers, or investors. Our market had to be educated to the wealth-accumulation and building process. I began working on plans to begin our learning process. I'm convinced that as more black people learn about the virtues of financial planning, saving, and investing, we will become participants in the financial-services industry and the benefits that could be achieved therein.

Promoters of diversity & inclusion should understand that doing so would experience the immediate cost benefit of receiving quality operations by including diverse talents with varying backgrounds, new and innovative ideas, and confidence. It would replenish the pipeline of the financial advisors who are rapidly leaving the industry with a well-trained, new, and effective workforce to meet the challenges of a rapidly changing economy.

Major impediments to the diversity/inclusion movement include:

- beliefs that diversity/inclusion success would reduce quality
- unconscious and overt biases
- the industry's excuse that they can't find qualified talent
- qualified talent does not believe industry will make necessary changes that consider new ideas and meet the needs of a changing global workforce
- changing structural industry emphasis on independent advisors who may only make hiring decisions based on profits and biases

- legislative decisions to appeal the Dodd-Frank Act and the fiduciary rule
- available talents are uncertain if the industry will make serious diversity & inclusion changes in the current political environment

Change must come from the top to the bottom, and top management must be intimately involved in the diversity & inclusion program. Top management should designate a specific office that will bring innovative thoughts and ideas directly to them and monitor any corrective actions that need to be taken. Efforts in this regard have already started. They should make a long-term commitment to the program by granting funds and other resources in partnership with outside organizations that are more involved in the groups being affected. Top management must not accept the myth that qualified diverse talent cannot be found. The industry must understand that a large potential talent pool already exists within one resource: HBCUs.

With that in mind, I founded a group of educated and well-trained financial advisors. The Association of African American Financial Advisors was actively involved in black communities, churches, and professional and social groups to support programs that improve our communities by teaching them how to save, invest, and improve their financial behaviors. AAAA members and HBCUs are definitely capable of narrowing the financial-services practitioner gap while using their abilities to reach the underserved and underrepresented.

In retrospect, it led me to question the industry proponents of diversity & inclusion and how committed they are to the movement. To make major steps forward, the industry need only to fund worthy organizations that could better reach and teach the industry's target audience while fulfilling their projected goals. The financial-services industry leaders are brilliant and successful professionals, and I find it hard to believe they do not see the benefits of including blacks and other minorities in their future plans.

It has been forecast that the African American spending power will be in excess of $1.2 trillion dollars by 2020. If we were a country, we would have the consumer spending power of Spain, which would be approximately the world's sixth highest consumer spender. If the industry could redirect 1 percent of the African American consumer spending power to savings and investments, it does not take a mathematical genius to see that that progress alone would be cost beneficial to the industry. This could happen if financial-services companies partnered with groups like AAAA to provide products and services to black people.

The D&I movement needs some partner angels in this march to reach the goals and objectives to close the employment gap, meet the demands of a changing workforce, be competitive, and improve the economic and social plight of African Americans. *InvestmentNews*, the leading information source for financial advisers, has committed to be a "drum major" by partnering with AAAA in this march.

*InvestmentNews* launched its inaugural Excellence in Diversity & Inclusion Lifetime Achievement Award, and Lazetta Rainy Braxton—CEO of Financial Fountain, chair of AAAA, and president of the AAAA Foundation—nominated me for the award. I was endorsed by Marilyn Mohman-Gillis,

CEO of the CFP® Board Center for Financial Planning for the award.

To my surprise and delight, I was chosen as the recipient of the award for my dedication to fostering a diverse financial-advice industry and commitment to increasing financial literacy. In recognition of the importance of diversity & inclusion, *InvestmentNews* made this inaugural award a special introduction for efforts to increase and promote diversity & inclusion in the advice business. This was definitely big news for me and for how it fit the vision and mission of God's ultimate plan for me. This is His award, and I thank Him for allowing me to share in the recognition.

The AAAA brand also needed broader exposure to continue its membership growth and its ability to help more people. The award helped accomplish that purpose.

My selection, vetting, interview cover photos, and video productions were thorough, and I enjoyed the process from start to finish. I first had to choose those who were to be interviewed (which were limited), share photos of my family and me, and share a pertinent biography of my life and career. All of this had to be approved by the *InvestmentNews* staff. Since I was already in the midst of writing this book, a great deal of the information was readily available. My selection was made in June, but I could not talk with others about the award until my story and video were released in the August 6 issue of *InvestmentNews*. How does one keep this history-making award secret from family, friends, peers, and associates for such a long time? It was difficult, but with the exception of my wife, I did it.

The culminating award event was spectacular. It was held on October 9, 2018, at the Edison Hotel Ballroom in New York City. In attendance, I had my AAAA members, their families, Randall Eley, investment manager of the Edgar Lomax Value Fund, Mt. Calvary Chair of the Trustee Ministry, Milton Harrison, and his wife, Sheila, professional peers, and my Good Samaritan, Alexandra Armstrong, who got me started in the financial planning industry.

More than two hundred people attended the event, and I thought the diversity & inclusion mission and recognition of the importance of purpose were received well. I was delighted to see the faculty and students of Delaware State in attendance. Reaching and motivating HBCU students on the importance and virtues of financial planning and how it can help African Americans and our communities is central to my mission.

# Chapter 20

# Advice to the Next Generation of African American Financial Advisors

I believe the financial-services industry will ultimately realize that partnering with AAAA or a similar organization will be a win-win affiliation for a new and changing workforce. The industry now sees that the income and wealth of African Americans is steadily growing while the industry current advisor numbers are shrinking, resulting in the fear of projected market loss. Recent reports indicate that there are more financial advisors over the age of seventy than those under fifty. I see opportunities for the next generation of African American advisors.

Some of these companies sincerely want to diversify the industry and include us in their future plans, and they could do so at very little financial cost. The expense needle on the profit and loss statement would not move much—if at all. African American advisors could help stop the bleeding and fill the pipeline with qualified advisors to sustain their profitability.

The financial-services and related industries have determined that the Certified Financial Planner designation is the gold standard for financial planners. Getting that designation should be at the top of any African American financial advisor's to-do list if we want to be marketable and seek employment or affiliation in the financial planning and advice industry.

If we want to be independent financial advisors or registered investment advisors, the industry-appropriate designations will enhance our chances for success. It will be difficult to succeed in the industry as a solo practitioner. We must take the team approach with capabilities in multiple disciplines within our practices to compete in today's financial-services industry. A successful financial advisor does not plan for yesterday or even today; the successful financial advisor plans for tomorrow.

The industry is constantly changing, and we must be prepared to change with it. Always be a student of your profession and develop strengths in a specific financial discipline, such as tax planning, estate planning, business law, or international finance. Determine your marketing base and decide what it will take to service them. You can build on your base later.

Be aware of your competition—and their pluses and minuses. Plan for your business as you would have your clients plan for their goals. Try to have multiple income centers in your firm so that tough times in one income stream will not close you down—financial plans, financial consultations, tax preparation, or tax planning—or if your marketing base plans need adjusting. Focus on the things you do well instead of the things you do not do well. For competition and your chances for promotion in your employment, identify the areas where you need strengthening and improve them.

To improve your weak areas, you must be a student of your profession and continue your financial education (formal or not) by participating in webinars and joining organizations such as AAAA and the AAAA Foundation where you can discuss and present current and forecasted economic trends. Keep in mind that your ultimate success may come from clients who are not part of your marketing base. It is better to be proactive than reactive in seeking success as a financial advisor—independent or not.

Be cognizant of your chosen expert opinions. Focus your improvement efforts on your marketing base first and relate the results directly to that base in planning your future practice strategy. For advisors who are employed or affiliated, you must integrate your strategy plans with the leading company. You must also realize that, in so doing, you become a company within a company and still must develop your personal planning strategy to maintain your employment or affiliation.

Words of Wisdom

"Without consultation, plans are frustrated, but with many counselors, they succeed" (Proverbs 15:22).

"The naïve man believes everything, but the prudent man considers his steps" (Proverbs 14:15).

Keep up the image at the line of scrimmage. Your appearance, attire, self-confidence, and presentation are all qualities that may determine whether you get a job or an affiliation. The employer or owner sets the criteria and the rules—not the employee or contractor.

The question should not be why plan but *how* to plan. Planning involves projecting months and years into the future based on your big three: *goals and objectives, time horizon,* and *risk tolerance.*

"The plans of the diligent lead to profit as sure as haste leads to poverty" (Proverbs 21:5).

When trying to get their business, future clients will be asking for the value we bring to the table. We must ask ourselves if we were in a room of peers trying to convince a prospect to choose us as their financial planner or advisor, why would they choose you?

"For which one of you, when he wants to build a tower, does not first sit down and calculate the cost, to see if he has enough to complete it?" (Luke 14:28).

A good financial advisor should have an opinion on any subject impacting the plans of their clients. It does not mean you will always be right, but you should be able to justify and discuss your opinion. Those you see or hear through mass media do the same thing. What you see or hear is just an opinion and not what you always need to know.

Statistics have proven that a large percentage of marriage discord, domestic abuse, and suicides come from the inability to properly handle financial problems.

Smart investors do not vet the investment—but the financial advisor. Bet on the jockey—not the horse. Good jockeys do not ride bad horses.

The stock market is not what it appears to be; it is what investors perceive it to be.

Always be a student of your profession and know how that knowledge applies to your clients or employer.

Financial advisors working for a company are like subsidiaries of a parent entity. You need your own business plan that fits within the parent's plan for long-term success.

Prof. Nandita Das, CFP®, my wife Jewel and Delaware State University (HBCU) and students at AAAA National Conference in Baltimore. Lanta Evans Motte, is on back row right. I'm on the back row left.

# Chapter 21

# RIAs and Robo Advisors

---

The financial advisory industry is constantly evolving, and we need to be flexible in planning for future career adjustments. At the top of the list is the Registered Investment Adviser (RIA) role in providing investment advice.

In taking a step back on my practice experience, I have seen the financial-advice industry arrive at some of the same points I have based my financial planning services on for more than forty years. As a fee-only planner, I have always felt that I was in compliance with current securities law as it applies to the fiduciary standard requirements. I am also a Maryland RIA, which allowed me to take steps forward in servicing my clients and building my practice

## RIA

The Registered Investment Adviser movement is rapidly increasing in popularity and execution. Some have projected that the RIA is the future of the financial advisory industry.

According to Wikipedia:

> A Registered Investment Adviser is a firm that is an investment advisor (spelled "investment adviser" in US financial law). An investment adviser is defined by the Securities and Exchange Commission as an individual or a firm that is in the business of giving advice about securities. However, an RIA is the actual firm, while the employees of the firm are called Investment Adviser Representatives (IARs).

An IAR must generally complete the Uniform Investment Adviser Law Examination (Series 65 exam) or meet the exam-waiver requirement by holding one or more of the following prequalifying designations: Certified Financial Planner (CFP®), Chartered Financial Consultant (ChFC), Personal Financial Specialist (PFS), Chartered Financial Analyst (CFA), or Chartered Investment Counselor (CIC). These requirements differ by states.

The Securities and Exchange Commission has regulatory authority over RIAs that manage more than $100 million. RIAs managing less than $100 million are usually regulated by the state of their operation. Usually the state's authority has been transferred to the Financial Advisory Regulatory Authority (FINRA). RIAs receive compensation from fees for providing financial advice and investment management and are required to act as fiduciaries.

Broker-dealers and their representative are not required to be fiduciaries, which presents a problem for small financial advisors and financial planners who charge commissions. However, fee-only planners and IARs can meet the fiduciary standards if they are structured and monitored properly. The fiduciary standard requires IAs to act and serve a client's best interests with the intent to eliminate or at least expose all potential conflicts of interest that might incline an IA—consciously or unconsciously—to render advice that was not in the best interest of the Investor Advisors' clients (US Investment Advisers Act of 1940).

In deciding to be an RIA or join an established one, there are compliance and insurance needs to consider in meeting the responsibility regulatory requirements. The RIA standards require constant monitoring, care, and maintenance and can be costly, which small firms should consider before pursuing independent RIA status. However, independent compliance firms are available to help you with the compliance requirements, and insurance professionals will design an asset-protection plan based on your needs.

Becoming an RIA could be rewarding and profitable, but if you are small, it may be advisable to be an IAR to gain valuable experience, increase your personal marketing base, and take advantage of the RIA research, marketing connections, and other resources.

Robo Advisors

Robo advisors are automated investment platforms that handle the construction and maintenance of an investment portfolio for you. You open an investment account and answer some questions about your goals and risk tolerance, and the platform invests your money in a preconstructed portfolio (typically a collection of low-cost ETFs).[2]

The portfolio is picked from ETFs that are part of the robo advisor's platform. The accounts are passively managed by the robo advisor. Market share is important to all financial advisors, but you have to be realistic in determining your market base without lowering your goals. Blind optimism will not suffice. Will robo advising shrink your market base?

There are some benefits and drawbacks to using robo advisors. I do not believe that new investors who have not begun to embrace or adopt good savings and investment habits will flock to robo advisors because they lack trust in the financial advisory industry and need personalized, face-to-face advice.

I believe integrating technology with the common touch to take time to discuss family affairs with children and relatives while delivering professional personal financial advice is the key to building a solid financial planning/advisory practice you can depend on. That has been my approach in developing a solid marketing base that has lasted me for decades.

The financial-advice industry is turning very quickly into managing people instead of just managing assets. That is how you build a long-term practice. A robo advisor does not provide that common touch. However, I do believe blending the common touch with technology, if handled with care, is the wave of the future of the industry.

---

[2] *The Simple Dollar,* February 26, 2019.

Benefits

- low-cost indexed portfolios
- user-friendly and offer portfolios that meet your goals and objectives, risk tolerance, and investor profile
- tax efficiency

These benefits will not help if your investments are held within 401(k)s, IRAs, or other retirement accounts, but they may be helpful when using a taxable account.

Drawbacks

- Robo advisors are not financial planners—even though some contend they are.
- They may not meet fiduciary standards.
- Portfolio investments may not meet your personalized goals and objectives, time horizon, and risk tolerance. Investment advice is one-step-fits-all advice.
- Client prospects may be reluctant to rely on investment advice by a machine and may desire a more hands-on, personal relationship with their investment advisor.
- They may cost more than the lowest cost all-in-one funds.
- They, like all investments, cannot guarantee performance.

Financial planners and advisors would be good employment candidates for robo advisors who could use them to expand their markets.

# Chapter 22

# My Ultimate Plan and HBCUs

Although many Historically Black Colleges and Universities are having financial problems, they should find some way to incorporate the many diversity & inclusion efforts of the financial-services industry in their future plans. The industry is making major strides in reaching out to HBCUs to help the industry deal with the gap being generated by the retiring and aging financial advisor pool. Diversity & inclusion programs are being promoted at a rapid pace, but they do not have the answers for how to do so. That is where HBCUs come into play.

Private industry could help fund the efforts. The combined efforts could be a win-win proposition for both parties. HBCUs must improve their financial management and accountability for the funds received from all sources to meet the standards and requirements of their resources because private industry will be watching and monitoring how those funds are administered.

The major efforts to reach HBCUs should be centered on the training, internships, employment, and industry experience of the students. If HCBUs could see substantial possibilities in those areas, there would be very little hesitancy to register with the CFP® Board of Standards requirements. If the industry could increase pledges and contributions to offset some of the costs, provide necessary training for the program, and underwrite the financial curriculum of the necessary staffing and administration, HCBUs would be eager to register with the CFP® Board of Standards.

Only a few HBCUs have met the registration requirements and entertained proposals to increase their numbers. Organizations such as the Association of African American Financial Advisors have some innovative ideas that could assist the CFP® Board of Standards in accelerating its success.

I took a step back and looked at my experience at Wilberforce and how it prepared me for my financial-services career. Some education does not come from books but from our historical backgrounds, intimate knowledge of our people and where we came from, and the development of our financial behavior.

God sent me to Wilberforce, and I saw, felt, and responded to the spiritual beliefs that have been a lamp to my footsteps and light unto my pathway as I progressed in my financial-services career. At Wilberforce, I saw students who had gone there to be messengers of Go; they were delivering mock sermons in the halls, on campus, and in the cafeteria to spread the Word of God. This made me stronger and more capable of withstanding the adversities I would eventually experience in life.

I believe matriculating at a HBCU institution could allow us to appreciate what our people went through and will face progressing and being inclusive in the financial-services industry. No matter how genuine and noble the efforts of private industry and other educational institutions, HBCUs' understanding of and compassion for our people could substantially accelerate the pace of successfully meeting the goals of diversity & inclusion of black people in the financial-services industry. Their involvement and partnership with private industry could be the genesis of a viable solution to the plight of God's people's social and economic problems.

What would the industry get out of such largesse besides doing what is just and right? Those companies that truly believe in diversity & inclusion would replenish the workforce pipeline and receive the benefits of a new innovative workforce that will be competitive in the future. Statistics have proven that the companies that improve the diversity of their workforce have also experienced growth in their net profits and increased their share market value. Understanding this win-win proposition is what this book and my ultimate plan are all about.

# Chapter 23

# Taking the Next Steps Forward

---

Anyone interested in becoming a professional financial planner should thoroughly investigate and research the industry. They should communicate with established organizations and get their opinions before making a decision: the Certified Board of Standards (CFP®), the CFP® Board Center for Financial Planning, the Financial Planning Association (FPA), the FPA Foundation, and the Association of African American Financial Advisors (AAAA). They should be concerned about who their members are and how their licensees are regulated. Compensation and transparency should be clearly understood. I took these steps and made sure financial planning fit my mission and vision before taking a step forward.

I knew I wanted to be a fee-only planner who would help my people understand what financial planning was and how it could help them prosper and earn enough to take care of their families and prepare their children for a better future. I did not plan for the past. I planned for the future of the financial planning industry—and I made adjustments along the way.

I identified my initial marketing base, as Dr. Ginsburgh prompted me to, and I began to build my practice on that base. My wife and I prepared our own financial plan because I wanted to practice what I preached. Did I want to work for a bank, a brokerage, or an insurance company—or be an independent planner? What were the pros and cons of each? How difficult would it be to build on my base? Who would be my chief competition? Those were some of the basics I had to grasp and accept before taking the plunge into a relatively new profession.

I was not looking for just a job. I had a well-paying and interesting job, but I wanted a career. Give me a fish and I eat for a day, but teach me how to fish, and I will eat for a lifetime. I was looking for a profession that could teach me for a lifetime and fit into my ultimate plan.

I researched an organization—the International Association for Financial Planning—that fit my requirements, and as God would have it, I met and was counseled by my initial financial planning mentor, Alexandra Armstrong, on how to eat for a lifetime. It was not easy, and I've been through some fire and rain, but I've made it thus far by the grace of God (see chapter 20 for my advice for the next generation of African American financial planners).

Advice for Those We Serve

Recent surveys have projected the consumer buying power of African Americans to be approximately $1.2 trillion dollars by the year 2021. If we can divert a small percentage of that spending power to savings and investing for ourselves, our families, and our communities, we can contribute so much good to our meeting increased health care costs, rising retirement needs, and crippling student debt.

Fellow African American financial advisors, take advantage of this season—and see how many clients you could have if you knew how to capture them. The financial advisory industry has a plan to benefit from the growing spending power, but they need African American advisors' help to capture a portion of the African American spending dollars. So, unite to share in the harvest.

We should use every financial and tax consultation and financial product sale and service as a teachable moment to our African American clients. If we are successful, those efforts could improve our future earnings and performance returns for our clients.

I caution my seminar attendees and readers of my articles to get to know how to choose a financial advisor. All potential clients should do their homework before choosing a financial advisor. Here are a few tips for selecting a financial advisor:

- Never retain a financial advisor who is not regulated by a reputable, well-known authority (SEC, FINRA, CFP® Board of Standards, etc.).
- Do not select a financial advisor solely because he or she is African American.
- Meet with the advisor, and if you feel comfortable with them and they are compliant with the professional standards, licensing, and regulations, then consider

retaining them. It may be wise to check FINRA's "Broker Check" if you are considering purchasing securities. A second opinion may also be in order.

- Be very careful about granting your financial advisor a full power of attorney. A limited power of attorney, which bars access to your withdrawals from your account, is preferable.

- Have your investment portfolio reviewed at least once a year if active, if it represents a major portion of your retirement assets, or if you depend on portfolio income to meet monthly expenses. The size of your portfolio should not necessarily determine the frequency of your portfolio review. Your investment and market activities should be taken into consideration when you determine that a portfolio review is necessary. If your goals and objectives, time horizon, or risk tolerance change, a review is recommended.

- The stock market will always go up and down. That's the definition of volatility. If you can't stand the motion, still the notion to invest.

- Do not respond to telephone or email investment solicitations without consulting with an independent financial advisor.

- If you do not understand or feel comfortable with the integrity and competence of an advisor, get a second opinion.

- Beware of scammers and financial abuse, especially for the elderly.

I have written this book to motivate and inspire the next generation of African American financial advisors who have an opportunity to better ourselves, our communities, and so many others from virtues of the financial planning profession. I hope this book inspires the next generation of African American financial advisors, our communities, and others who will benefit from their counsel.

# Chapter 24

# The Best Client I Ever Had

---

God is the best client I ever had. He invested His blessings in me and expects and deserves a return on His investment. The return He expects is not money or material things. The world and all that dwell within are already His. His time horizon is infinite. Whosoever believes in Him shall not die but have everlasting life.

There is no risk when you keep your hand in His hand. He demands that we tell the world about His Love, His Works, His Will, and His Word. He expects me to tell others what He has done for me and will do for them if they just believe in Him and follow Him. He wants me to spread His love to all—even to my enemies—and to do unto others as I would have them do unto me. He will monitor my performance, admonish me when I do poorly, and continue blessing me when I am obedient to His Word.

My early years community basketball
team. That's me on the top row left

The Davis family. I am in the center, top row
with Garland and LeCount, Jr. Bottom row is
Felandria, Michelle and wife Jewel on the right.

LeCount and Jewel Honeymoon in Bermuda
June 1965

Family Home in Potomac, MD for 39 years
Memories like the corners of our minds

Author and Maryland Comptroller, Peter Franchot
at Family & Financial Literacy Workshop

Thomas Bastian, President BHCAWU Workers and I
visiting the Bank construction site in the Bahamas

I made a visit to the newly opened Bahamas
BHCAWU Workers Bank

H Miller President and CEO of
Social and Scientific Systems

Randall Eley Investment Manager, Founder
and CEO of the Edgar Lomax Co.

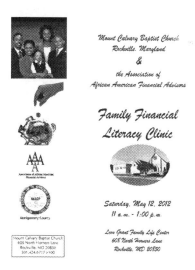

Mt. Calvary Baptist Church and the
Nicholsons, the 1st family representatives of
the Family Financial Literacy Ministry

I congratulated speakers of a Mt. Calvary Baptist Church Family Financial Literacy Seminar for a job well done. Daphane Wright CPA, CFP and Russell Price MBA, CPA Accounting and Tax professionals

Drew Byrd (left) and Howard Nicholson (right) young attendees of a Mt. Calvary Financial Literacy Program Courtesy of John Davis church photographer for FFLM

Lanta Evans Motte, past AAAA
president and Board Member

Attendees of The Family & Financial Litracy Workshop

# Endorsements

"LeCount has been a leader in the financial services industry for decades. His life's story is an inspiration not only to many in the Washington, DC community, but to business leaders throughout the Nation. It's well worth your time to read this wonderful biography by a true American icon."

-- George L. Garrow, Jr. Esq.

One Step Back, Two Steps Forward conveys the wisdom and perspective of Lecount R. Davis who has been a trailblazer in the field of financial planning for over 35 years. Lecount has introduced the concepts and principles of financial planning to hundreds of persons. He has also provided leadership and guidance to a whole generation of African American financial advisors hoping to follow in his footsteps. Through a combination of public education, advocacy and professional practice, he has been a champion for the use of financial planning as a tool for the achievement of personal life goals as well as overall community economic development. The book recounts how his life journey has influenced his approach to individual and collective wealth building in spite of the many obstacles faced by the vast majority of the population.

His focus on the use of time-tested financial management strategies to achieve realistically conceived goals provides a blueprint for all who are overwhelmed by the financial complexities of modern life.

-- Jeffery A. Hunter CPA. CFP®, CSA®

LeCount Davis, CFP® has been a mentor to me for about six years. In an industry full of egos, Mr. Davis is one of the most down to earth, successful individuals I have met. He is never too busy to provide council and to share his opinion, whether you ask for it or not. When he speaks you better listen because he speaks from a place of spirituality and knowledge. Mr. Davis has helped me to me a more successful advisor and has challenged me to mentor younger advisors just starting out in this business.

-- Nicolas T. Abrams, CFP®

# Epilogue

If we want to truly make a difference in the economic plight and financial struggle of the massive number of the underserved population, we must reach them and teach them the advantages of earning a living, taking care of our families, saving, and investing. In making our educational and vocational choices, we will need to know how to be good stewards of God's many blessings if we are to meet the challenges we face in our families, our neighborhoods, and our charitable giving pursuits. Believing this greatly influenced me in choosing my financial planning career and writing this book. My experiences and employment history could be repeated by many people who will not choose to pursue a career in the financial-services industry, but they could benefit from the advantages of financial planning in their lives and raising their children to be the best they can be.

No matter how dire the circumstances, you can always find hope in the hands of God. Sometimes the challenge is financial, such as when the money does not stretch to the end of the month, employee problems, economic downturns, or family problems.

In our financial dance of life's journey, we must make adjustments and do things that we feel are necessary to compensate for our adversities. We should always have options and backup plans for when adversity occurs—even if you do not like the options.

When you want to know what to do and how to do it these days, you go to the internet and google the subject you seek for help. When I sought the guidance, perseverance and steps for my ultimate plan, I went to the greatest life instruction book ever written – the BIBLE.

# About the Author

LeCount R. Davis is a Certified Financial Planner (CFP®) and a Registered Investment Adviser in Maryland (RIA). He is the chairman emeritus for the Association of African Financial Advisors (AAAA) and chairman of the AAAA Foundation. He lives in Potomac, Maryland, with his wife, Jewel, and she has been the wind beneath his wings for more than fifty-three years.

He is dedicated to his vision and mission that God blessed him with the vision and mission to provide the African American people with the financial guidance and advice to improve their social and economic conditions. He believes that the lack of proper financial stewardship is the genesis of our social and economic problems that we face today: family discord, divorce, domestic abuse, crime, and death.

He has a BCS and MCS accounting degrees from Southeastern University in Washington, DC, and a diploma from the College for Financial Planning in Denver, Colorado. He was the first black person to receive the Certified Financial Planning designation (CFP®). He served as an adjunct accounting professor at Howard University in Washington,

DC. He also served as the independent investment consultant for the Bahamas Hotel and Allied Industries and the Bahamas Hotel Management Pension Funds.

His recognitions and awards include:

- 2018 *InvestmentNews* Inaugural Excellence in Diversity & Inclusion Lifetime Achievement Award
- 2018 Society for Financial Education and Professional Development (SFE&PD) Eagle Award
- 2008 National Capital Area (NCA) Lifetime Achievement Award
- 2008 Mt. Calvary Baptist Church Sam Chapman Heart for Men Award
- Association of African American Financial Advisors (AAAA) founder, chairman emeritus, and board member
- IAFP National Capital Chapter (now known as the Financial Planning Association) past president (1983) and board member
- Mt. Calvary Baptist Church Family Financial Literacy, ministry chairman
- 2000 Alpha Kappa Alpha TOO Chapter Community Service Award for Blazing New Trails in Economics
- 2015 National Council of Negro Women—Montgomery County, Maryland Section, Recognition of Service in Financial Management to Churches, Individuals, and Nonprofit Organizations
- Former host of the Howard University TV (WHMM now WHUT)—*Common Cents* business program

- Author and publisher of "Finance and the African American Family" newsletter
- Cambridge Who's Who February 2, 2007, lifetime member
- 1975–1976 and 2019 Marquis "Who's Who in Finance and Industry"
- 2019 Alpha Kappa Alpha TOO Chapter Community Service Award for Contribution and Excellence in Building Your Economics Legacy

# Endorsements

LeCount's life story is truly motivating. He has been a pioneer and role model for all financial planners—not just African Americans. His book is an inspiration and must-read for any aspiring new financial planner but also for corporate executives of planning firms who are committed to increasing diversity among their planners. If they take his advice, they will be successful.

—Alexandra Armstrong, CFP®, CRPC, chairman
and founder, Armstrong, Fleming & Moore Inc.

LeCount's story is a story that is meant to be shared. His professional achievements as a pioneer in his profession have served to inspire those who have come behind him. In times when many are trying to emulate others and discover their secret sauce for success, LeCount sees fit to offer a truth-telling message about his journey. LeCount is often affectionally referred to as the "The Godfather" by some of us who have been joined together through the Association of African American Financial Advisors. But with utmost humility through this writing, he makes attribution that it is his Almighty Father to whom he credits for his achievements.

This book is far more than an inside peek into the life and journey of an esteemed and legendary trailblazer; it is an inspiring read that can encourage anyone with dreams, focus, and faith.

—Daphne Wright, CPA, CFP®

LeCount Davis is the personification of faith, determination, and flexibility. We met in late 1986, over lunch, shortly after I founded the Edgar Lomax Company, and I was immediately impressed with his singular focus and his apparent goodwill toward me and my work. The past more than thirty years of discussions, interactions, and sometimes collaborations have only increased my respect for the strong work ethic and positive attitude he brings to every project. LeCount's story provides lessons, and therefore is a must-read for anyone who wishes to succeed—even in the face of adversity—in finance, or anyone who simply wishes to live an orderly and successful life in the midst of what is often a disorderly world.

—Randall Eley, founder and CEO of
the Edgar Lomax Company

Printed in the United States
By Bookmasters